How to Raise Confident Children

How to Raise
Confident
Children

Richard L. Strauss

BAKER BOOK HOUSE
Grand Rapids, Michigan 49506

Library of Congress Catalog Card Number: 75-7225.
ISBN: 0-8010-8239-0
Copyright © 1975
Tyndale House Publishers, Inc.,
Wheaton, Illinois 60187.

Reprinted 1984 by Baker Book House with permission of copyright owner.

Formerly published under the title *Confident Children and How They Grow.*

Printed in the United States of America.

To Steve, Mike, Mark, and Tim
Charter members of the
"Keep Dad Humble Club"
and the joy of their father's heart

My son, if your heart is wise,
My own heart also will be glad;
And my inmost being will rejoice,
When your lips speak what is right.
Proverbs 23:15, 16, NASB

Contents

How to Raise
Confident
Children

Before You Read On...

You should know that I really wanted to wait until all our children were grown before I wrote this book. Maybe then (if they all turn out well) you would view me as an expert on the subject of child rearing. But I decided I could not wait that long. I need this book now. You see, this is an examination and explanation of another book, the best one ever written on the subject of raising children, *God's Guidebook for Child Rearing*, the Bible.

When I began this study each of our four sons was on a different educational level—one in college, one in high school, one in junior high, and one in elementary school. My wife and I began to realize how rapidly time flies and how little we have left in which to influence their lives. We decided that we need a more thorough understanding and a more consistent application of God's rules for successful child rearing *now* so that our kids *will* turn out right. And so this book! The study has made a tremendous difference in our home life. It is our prayer that it will be every bit as helpful to yours.

But I must be quick to add, we are a long way from being perfect. And reading this book isn't going to transform you into a perfect parent overnight either. God's principles must be put into practice. As we come into an understanding of his Word we must obey it, and this will require some changes in our way of thinking and way of living. As the Lord shows you things that need to be changed, jot them down. Ask him to give you the commitment and the courage to do something about them. You will be tempted to continue to do things the same way you have always done them. It's the easiest way to go. It takes a deep desire and dogged determination to change. But God is in the business of building that kind of motivation into the lives of those who want it and seek it. "For God is at work within you, helping you want to obey him, and then helping you do what he wants."[1]

That presupposes, of course, that the Spirit of the living Christ does dwell in your life. The Bible says he lives in the life of every true Christian, you know. "And remember that if anyone doesn't have the Spirit of Christ living in him, he is not a Christian at all."[2] This is a book for Christian parents who want to establish a truly Christian home.

Maybe that term "Christian home" demands a word of explanation. It isn't necessarily a home where a picture of Jesus hangs on the wall and a family Bible lies on the coffee table. It isn't even a home where grace is always said before meals and the family members attend church regularly, as valuable as those things are. It is a home where folks have acknowledged their sinfulness and have trusted the Lord Jesus Christ as their Savior from the guilt and penalty of sin. Or as Jesus put it, they have been born again.[3] They have received the gift of eternal life by faith in him,[4] and the love of God now fills and remodels their lives.[5]

For Christian parents seeking to establish a Christian home, divine direction and supernatural help are available. The Bible provides the guidance and the Holy Spirit supplies the strength. And in addition to that, God is infinitely gracious. Mary and I can testify to that. As this edition goes to press, our four sons continue to go on with the Lord in spite of our mistakes. They all have their weaknesses, but they keep bringing us more joy than we ever could have imagined. The final verdict is not yet in but we are trusting God to continue the good work he has begun.

With those issues settled, we are ready to get on with our study. If our minds are open to God's Word and our wills are submissive to his control, there are joyous days ahead for our families.

[1]Philippians 2:13, TLB
[2]Romans 8:9b, TLB
[3]John 3:3, 7
[4]John 3:16
[5]Romans 5:5

1

Blessing or Bother

How could I ever forget the birth of our first child? It was early in the morning and I was rather groggy, but even through the fog of the years I can still project on the screen of my mind some vivid scenes from my memory bank. I remember telling Mary to go back to sleep. The baby wasn't due yet. She wouldn't cooperate! I can still see the doctor walking toward me in the hallway of the hospital, looking like a giant pea pod in his surgical greens, announcing with a note of happy triumph, "It's a boy!" He know what I was rooting for.

Little did I realize it at the moment, but I would hear that very same announcement three more times, each with a little less of the happy triumph. After all, variety is the spice of life, and what father in his right mind doesn't want a little girl to put her arms around his neck and say, "I love you, Daddy." I have learned, however, that God knows far better than I do what my needs are. Since he gave me those boys, and since they are exactly what I need for my own spiritual growth and blessing, no human being could make me give any

one of them up of my own volition. Next to the wonderful wife the Lord has given me, they are the most precious things in this world to me. Those beautiful words of the ancient poet of Israel have taken on new meaning:
> Lo, children are a heritage of the Lord:
> and the fruit of the womb is his reward.
> As arrows are in the hand of a mighty man;
> so are children of the youth.
> Happy is the man who hath his quiver full of them.[1]

It is quite obvious that somebody wrote that a long time ago. There are not many people in twentieth-century America with the Psalmist's viewpoint on children. A modern version might sound more like this:
> Lo, children are a burden from the Lord;
> and the fruit of the womb must be his way of testing us.
> As the source of endless work and continual aggravation,
> so are the children of one's youth.
> Unhappy is the man who hears his neighbor ask,
> "Do all those kids belong to you?"

We can understand why folks might feel that way. Many children are rebellious, disobedient, disrespectful, and unmannerly—not very pleasant to be around. It's no wonder that some people have decided not to have any at all. What has gone wrong? Where did we lose God's perspective? The first verse of Psalm 127 may provide us with a clue. "Except the Lord build the house, they labor in vain that build it." Stable and successful homes are built by God. He is the architect and the general contractor. He has drawn the blueprint, and he wants to provide the direction and give the orders. All he needs are some laborers—husbands, wives and children—who will study the blueprint provided in his Word, then follow his directions. Any other procedure is going to result in frustration and failure.

---

[1]Psalm 127:3-5a, KJV

The basic problem in many homes is that we have departed from God's blueprint and have substituted man's. God is no longer the architect and builder. We are following instead the blueprint drawn by psychiatrists, psychologists, modern educators, doctors, and even syndicated columnists. Much of the advice we get from these sources is good. But if some parts of a blueprint are good and other parts are faulty, the result is going to be a weak building. The Bible is still the best textbook ever written on rearing children. We need to find out what it says and obey it. "Except the Lord build the house, they labor in vain that build it."

It is gratifying to note an increasing alarm about the situation. Newspaper and magazine articles, along with a growing number of books on the subject, are warning people of the dangers of an unhappy home and are trying to help them repair the damage. The information may be helpful, but unless people are willing to turn their hearts and homes over to the Lord, it may be too little too late. Listen to the Psalmist again. "Except the Lord keep the city, the watchman waketh but in vain." No ancient city was safe from attack no matter how thick its walls nor alert its guards unless God was protecting it. Likewise, no home is safe from the attack of Satan unless it has been consciously committed to the Lord, unless he has been put in charge. The homes where Jesus Christ reigns as Lord in the lives of every family member are the homes that will tower above the rest in love, serenity, happiness, mutual concern one for another, and the ability to adjust to people outside the home.

Some folks think there are other ways to produce a happy home. For example, "Work, work, work, as hard as you can. Provide all the material things of this world for your children. Maybe that will make them happy." If dad doesn't make enough money to do it, mom goes to work too. Read on in

Psalm 127. "It is vain for you to rise up early, to sit up late, to eat the bread of sorrows; for so he giveth his beloved sleep." The bread of sorrows is simply bread secured through toil and trouble. Food is essential, but God can provide it without taking fathers and mothers away from their children day and night to pursue that elusive and almighty dollar. God has no time for laziness. He blesses honest work, but he can supply the things we need without anxious efforts and ceaseless self-activity. The Psalmist says God provides for his beloved ones, literally, "in sleep," the idea being in calm, restful, confident trust in him.

The society in which we live has perverted our perspective. We have been sold a bill of goods, the false theory that we owe our children all the things they want. We hear parents say, "But we want them to have all the things we never had." So they have things, but they don't know who they are, or why they are here, or what they ought to accomplish in life. The most incorrigible rebels in our society are not necessarily the underprivileged. They are kids who have had all that money can buy but were never loved, appreciated, and accepted. They are empty and lonely on the inside because nobody has ever really cared for them or tried to understand them. They never had a warm and loving relationship with their parents. Many of them don't really know their parents, and furthermore they don't care to. Their parents don't know them either. They were too busy making money and having fun to listen to what their kids were saying. And so, we're told, the younger generation is facing an identity crisis. They're crying for attention, groping for some sort of significant relationship with somebody who cares. The saddest thing is that this is happening in professing Christian homes as well as in unbelieving homes. What is the answer?

The answer begins with believing what God says right here in this Psalm and acting on the basis of it. "Lo, children are a heritage of the Lord." The word *heritage* signifies an inheritance given, not according to hereditary right, but according to the willing desire of the giver. Every new child born into a Christian home is a gracious gift from God, a lovely legacy from the Lord entrusted to our care to be loved, cherished, provided for and properly molded for his glory. "The fruit of the womb is his reward." Again, the word *reward* does not mean something earned or deserved, but something freely given through the generous decision of the giver. The inability to have children is no stigma, therefore. It doesn't mean God is angry with us or isn't smiling on us. It simply means that he knows best what we need. And he also knows there are the masses of unloved children whom childless couples can pour their lives into with great spiritual profit for all concerned. He always gives what is best.

But when he allows us to have children, they are a gracious gift from him. There is no question about that when we stand over the crib and stare down at our beautiful bundle of joy, peacefully sleeping or contentedly cooing. We may begin to wonder a little about it during those first 2:00 A.M. feedings. And the doubts may really balloon if that little bundle of joy becomes a threatening intruder who upsets our schedule, restricts our freedom to do as we please, monopolizes our time, or seems to alienate the affections of our mate. That's when we need to flee to the Word, and to the Lord of the Word, to have our spirits encouraged and our perspective adjusted. Children are a heritage from the Lord.

Maybe you are well on your way down the precarious path of parenthood. When you look at your child, what do you see? A nerve-shattering machine, or a heritage from the Lord? A house-wrecker, or a heritage from the Lord? A work-maker, or a heritage from the Lord? A source of embarrassment before your friends, or a heritage from the Lord? A competitor for your spouse's attention, or a heritage from the Lord? Will you ask God to help you get your perspective straight? "Lord, help me see my children as a blessed gift from your gracious hand." You may need to pray it many times a day for awhile, but that could become the beginning of some exciting new changes in your home, the gateway to genuine joy in your relationship with your children.

Children are much more sensitive to our attitude toward them than we imagine. And they often respond with the same sort of attitudes they receive. They act as they sense we are acting toward them, and that's where most of our discipline problems begin. Oh, we love them, but they make so many demands on us that inconvenience us and bother us. So our old natures rebel and we let them know in subtle little ways that they are a bother. And they become more of a bother. They won't get much love and affection that way, but at least they'll get attention, and that's better than nothing. But they will grow up with hostilities, complexes, and resentments that defy description.

One day sooner than we think they'll be gone, and we won't remember the muddy shoes, the messy rooms, the embarrassing moments they caused us or the encroachments they made on our time. We'll only remember the happy times we spent together. And we'll wish there had been many more. There could have been if we had looked on them as a blessing from the Lord rather than a burden or a bother.

Children are not only a precious inheritance, however. They are also likened to arrows. There is a difference of opinion as to what this scriptural metaphor is intended to teach. Arrows are a source of protection, and maybe the Psalmist was referring to the care and protection which children can give their parents in later years. But arrows, unlike swords, could go where the warrior himself could not reach. Such is the case with our children. From many a godly home arrows have reached to the ends of the earth, carrying the gospel message to sin-darkened hearts.

While I was pastoring in Fort Worth, Texas, it was my privilege to get to know an old warrior of the cross named W. E. Hawkins. He had founded the church I was serving, and was at that time engaged in a radio ministry in Dallas. Many lives were being affected for the Savior through his efforts, but he was restricted primarily to the Southwest United States. W. E. Hawkins and his wife had three sons, all of whom went to the mission field. Through the ministry of those boys, primitive South American Indians whom their father could never reach came to know Jesus Christ. They were like arrows in their father's hand.

But arrows have to be made. They don't just happen. God gives us a child like a raw piece of wood, and asks us to shape him. So we whittle, sand, and polish, fashioning that stick into an arrow, straight and strong. Children are not just an inheritance, you see; they are a sacred trust. God loans them to us for awhile to prepare them for his use. They really belong to him, and the sooner we acknowledge that, the more willing we shall become to get on with the shaping process. One dramatic way of acknowledging it is to dedicate them to God. If they belong to him anyway, then let us decisively acknowledge that by consecrating them to his use for his glory just as Hannah and Elkanah did with their son, Samuel.[2] Let us promise God that with his help we will mold their young lives into the kind of people he wants them to be.

A husband and wife ought to give their child to God even before he is born. And they should pray together after the birth of the child, willingly dedicating themselves to train him as God directs. Some churches conduct public child dedication services. In others, the pastor participates in a quiet act of dedi-

[2]1 Samuel 1:9-28

cation in the home. The important thing is that the parents themselves covenant with God to handle their children as a sacred trust, arrows to be shaped for God's glory.

Raising children is obviously a serious responsibility. And isn't it strange—for almost any other job we are required to take some specialized training first. But for the most important business in life, the shaping of young lives for God's glory, we can get away with none at all if we want to. For that reason some people have drawn the erroneous conclusion that being a good parent comes naturally. On the contrary, it takes a great deal of study and continuous attention to the assignment. But God's guidebook is available, and we are going to search it for the help we need. Since this is one job we can't quit, we might as well press on together and learn what God has to say about being a better parent.

Before we do, though, will you note the last verse in this great Psalm? "Happy is the man who hath his quiver full of them: they shall not be ashamed, but they shall speak with the enemies in the gate." How many children constitute a full quiver? That may vary with each couple depending on how many children God wants you to have. My quiver is full at four, but yours is between you and the Lord. It isn't clear in the verse exactly who will not be ashamed, the parents or the children. But in a Christ-controlled home where God is the builder and parents are laboring for him, neither the parents nor the children will be ashamed of each other. But Satan, the enemy of God's people, will be subdued and God will thus be glorified. Isn't that what you desire for your family? Dedicate yourself and your children to God. Ask him to help you view them as a precious inheritance, arrows to be shaped, lives to be molded. Ask him to keep your eyes on the potential rather than the problems and to give you the wisdom you need for the great task ahead.

2
The Model Parent

Why does God give parents to children? With family troubles intensifying, discipline problems increasing, and a growing corps of psychologically handicapped people coming through the ranks of the traditional family circle, we wonder why God doesn't come up with a different way of bringing children to maturity than using parents in a home environment.

And he keeps them there so long, nearly eighteen years on the average. Most birds and animals mature and move out on their own in a matter of weeks or months. But the frequent failures of teen-age marriages dramatically illustrate that fifteen, sixteen, or even seventeen years may not be enough to prepare humans to establish successful homes of their own. Why?

Because, among other things, life for an animal is a matter of instincts which are basically inborn. Life for humans goes far beyond that. It involves intellectual and emotional character, volitional choices, moral and aesthetic values. These things are not instinctive; they are developed, and that takes time. God gives parents to children to help build the qualities into them that will prepare them for a most useful and satisfying life.

Other organizations and agencies also contribute to molding the character and personality of children, but none has the same degree of influence as their parents. This is due not only to the uniqueness and intensity of the parent-child relationship, but also to the sheer volume of time logged in the home. Before entering school, nearly all of our children's time is spent at home. Even during their school years, as many as sixty waking hours per week are spent in or around the home, far exceeding the hours spent in any other single place. What transpires during those hours will largely determine the kind of adults our children become, and the mark of those years will be indelibly imprinted on their personalities. God says a person's ways later in life will be determined by his early experiences and training.[1] Modern psychologists, sociologists, and educators agree. Our children are what we make them. They are the sum total of what we contribute to their lives. The training we provide will affect their ability to get along with other people, the genuineness of their Christian testimony and service, the caliber of work they do, the quality of home they establish, and almost every other area of their lives.

That's a staggering thought. Raising a child successfully sounds like a superhuman task. As a matter of fact, it is. It demands more than human resources have to offer. It requires supernatural wisdom and strength. "But I'm not God," you say. Right! Your children probably know that already. But God does promise to supply all your need.[2] And he knows exactly what you do need to be a good parent, because he himself is the Model Parent.

Isn't it interesting that when Jesus prayed he addressed God as "our Father, who art in heaven." God is a father. And the

[1]Proverbs 22:6
[2]Philippians 4:19

Psalmist exclaimed, "What a God he is! How perfect in every way!"[3] The obvious conclusion is that God is a perfect father. By examining his Word and learning how he functions as a parent, we can learn what kind of parents we should be. Then when we commit ourselves completely to him and let him control our lives, he is free to express through us his wisdom and strength as the Model Parent. He provides both the example and the encouragement, both the direction and the dynamic for us to be successful parents.

There are a number of Scripture passages that compare God's parenthood to ours. For example, the Psalmist wrote, "He is like a father to us, tender and sympathetic to those who reverence him."[4] Solomon made this wise observation which the writer to the Hebrews borrowed: "For whom the Lord loves He reproves, even as a father the son in whom he delights."[5] Jesus added his inspired testimony: "And if you hard-hearted, sinful men know how to give good gifts to your children, won't your Father in heaven even more certainly give good gifts to those who ask him for them?"[6]

The point is well established in the Bible. God's parenthood and our parenthood are a great deal alike—*at least they should be.* But did you notice that in all these verses the direction is from the human to the divine. Each verse uses human parents and the way they treat their children to teach us what God is like. Christian counselors have discovered that it does indeed work that way. A person's image of God is often patterned after his image of his own parents, especially his father. If his parents were happy, loving, accepting, and forgiving, he finds it easier to experience a positive and satisfying relationship with God. But if his parents were cold and indifferent, he may feel that God is far away and disinterested in him personally. If his parents were angry, hostile, and rejecting, he often feels that God can never accept him. If his parents were hard to please, he

---

[3]Psalm 18:30, TLB
[4]Psalm 103:13, TLB
[5]Proverbs 3:12, NASB;
   cf. Hebrews 12:6
[6]Matthew 7:11, TLB

usually has the nagging notion that God is not very happy with him either.

We need to meditate on that, Christian parent. What kind of God-concept is our child cultivating by his relationship with us? Is he learning that God is loving, kind, patient, and forgiving? Or are we unintentionally building a false image of God into his life, implying by our actions that God is harsh, short-tempered, and critical, that he nags us, yells at us, or knocks us around when we get out of line? Our children's entire spiritual life is at stake here. It is imperative that we learn what kind of a parent God is, then follow his example in order that our children may see a living object lesson of the kind of God we have.

There is at least one passage in the Bible, however, that does move from the divine to the human, exhorting us to follow God's example in raising our children. "And, fathers, do not provoke your children to anger; but bring them up in the discipline and instruction of the Lord."[7] Those three little words at the conclusion of this verse will set our course through the remainder of this book. The training we give our children must be the training "of the Lord." The Lord must be the guiding principle of that training. It belongs to him and is to be administered by him. It is the same training he gives us, and we are to give it to our children by his direction, through his power, under his authority, and answerable to him. It is "of the Lord" in every sense of that phrase. When we get right down to specific principles of child-training, the Bible does not have a great deal to say directly. But when we understand the great principle established in this verse, the Bible becomes an inexhaustible sourcebook for successful child training.

It boils down simply to this—we deal with our children as the Lord deals with us. He is our model. And our understanding of how he deals with us does not necessarily come from our parents, for that understanding may be faulty, as we have seen.

7Ephesians 6:4, NASB

It must come from his Word. We need to search the Scriptures to find out how God deals with his children, then do the same with our children.

Paul uses two words in Ephesians 6:4 to sum up God's method of rearing children—*discipline* and *instruction*. The first of these is a very general word for child-training. It involves setting goals for our children, teaching them the goals, then patiently but persistently guiding them toward those goals. While the word did not originally mean correction, it came through usage to include that idea and is translated "chastening" in Hebrews 12:5-7 (KJV). But discipline, contrary to popular opinion, is far more than correction. It is charting a course for our children, guiding them along that course, and firmly but lovingly bring them back to that course when they stray.

Think about charting the course for a moment. Have you ever prayerfully established goals for the training of your children? This might be a good time to do it. We cannot expect our children to turn out right if we're not sure what "right" is. As one of my seminary profs used to say, "If you aim at nothing, that's exactly what you'll hit." Since we can't hit a target we don't have, let's build one right now. Your aims may be much more extensive than mine, but this may at least be a good place to begin. Here is a basic list of biblical goals we want to accomplish with our children.

1. *To lead them to a saving knowledge of Jesus Christ.* It must be in his own perfect time, but we cannot really expect them to be all that God wants them to be until they have a new nature imparted from above.

2. *To lead them to a total commitment of their lives to Christ.* We want them to make their decisions in accord with his will, share every detail of life with him in prayer, and learn to trust him in every experience they face. Asking first what

God wants us to do is a habit pattern that must be cultivated. The time to begin is very early in a child's life.

3. *To build the Word of God into their lives.* We will endeavor to teach it to them faithfully, relate it to the circumstances of life, and set an example of conformity to it.

4. *To teach them prompt and cheerful obedience, and respect for authority.* By developing their willing submission to our authority, we seek to instill a respect for all duly constituted authority, such as public school, Sunday school, government, and ultimately, the authority of God himself. Submission to authority is the basis for a happy and peaceful life in our society.

5. *To teach them self-discipline.* The happiest life is the controlled life, particularly in areas such as eating, sleeping, sex, care of the body, use of time and money, and desire for material things.

6. *To teach them to accept responsibility*—responsibility for happily and efficiently accomplishing the tasks assigned to them, responsibility for the proper care of their belongings, and responsibility for the consequences of their actions.

7. *To teach them the basic traits of Christian character,* such as honesty, diligence, truthfulness, righteousness, unselfishness, kindness, courtesy, consideration, friendliness, generosity, justice, patience, and gratitude.

Now we know where we're going. But remember, our purpose is not just to insist on these things while our children are under our care. It is to make this whole package such a part of their lives that when they leave our care it will continue to guide them. That seems to be what Solomon had in mind when he wrote, "Young man, obey your father and your mother. Tie their instructions around your finger so you won't forget. Take to heart all of their advice. Every day and all night long their counsel will lead you and save you from harm; when you wake up in the morning, let their instructions guide you into the new day. For their advice is a beam of light directed into the dark corners of your mind to warn you of danger and to give you a good life."[8]

Internalizing these standards, that is, making them an integral part of the child's life, seems to be indicated in the second word Paul used in Ephesians 6:4 to describe the training God gives which we are to emulate, the word *instruction*. This word means literally, "to place in the mind." The emphasis is on verbal training—warning, admonishing, encouraging, instructing, or reproving. But it goes far beyond the famous parental lecture. It pictures the faithful parent tenderly planting the principles of God's Word deep down in the very soul of the child so that they become a vital part of his being. The standard is no longer the parent's alone. It now belongs to the child as well. He is ready to move out into the world, independent of his parent's control, with the principles of God's Word so woven into the fiber of his life that he finds delight and success in doing the will of God, even when nobody is watching him. Maybe this explains why some parents are reluctant to let go of their children when they should. If parents suspect they have not successfully instilled God's way of life into their children, they may hesitate to break their emotional ties with them, but seek to influence and manipulate them in various ways long after they have married and left home. God wants us to begin building toward independence from the time our children are born.

Parental rules, regulations, and restrictions are only temporary. Their purpose is to prepare the child for freedom, the only kind of freedom that can bring him real satisfaction, the freedom to live in harmony and happiness with his Maker and Lord. As he learns and matures, the restraints are decreased and the independence increased until he leaves our care to

---

[8]Proverbs 6:20-23, TLB

establish a home of his own, a self-disciplined, Spirit-directed adult, capable of assuming his God-given responsibilities in life.

This whole process is beautifully illustrated by the way God has dealt with the human race through the ages of history. In the time of man's spiritual childhood, God gave him the law— 613 commandments, ordinances, and judgments regulating nearly every detail of life. It isn't the way most people would choose to live, but it certainly did the job. Paul said, "The law was our schoolmaster to bring us unto Christ, that we might be justified by faith. But after that faith is come, we are no longer under a schoolmaster."[9] He goes on to describe the fullness of faith, the freedom of life in Christ, and the joy of adult sonship. Who needs the bondage of all those external laws when we have the internal motivation of the Holy Spirit?[10]

That's exactly what human parents should be doing. During the childhood years we regulate behavior while we inculcate biblical standards. As the child develops an inner discipline and control, more and more of the outward restrictions are removed until he has achieved the independence God intended him to have when he said, "Therefore shall a man leave his father and mother, and shall cleave unto his wife...."[11]

There are few joys in this world that excel the thrill of watching our children live in fellowship with God of their own willing desire. The Apostle John said, "I have no greater joy than to hear that my children walk in truth."[12] He was probably speaking of his spiritual children, but the idea is equally applicable to our physical children. Old Jacob must have had that joy when he heard the story of his son's encounter with Potiphar's wife. She offered Joseph her body and nobody would have been the wiser. Dad was several hundred miles away and it was doubtful at that point whether Joseph would ever see him again. But the godly principles built into his soul

[9]Galatians 3:24, 25, KJV
[10]cf. Galatians 4:1-7;
    Romans 8:14
[11]Genesis 2:24, KJV
[12]3 John 4, KJV

through his early years kept him from sin.[13]

Daniel's parents experienced that same joy if they ever heard of their son's steadfast devotion to God in Babylon. He was nearly six hundred miles from home. And all the other boys were gorging themselves with the sumptuous foods of the Babylonian king which had been dedicated to pagan idols. "Everybody else is doing it" and "Nobody will ever know" have been good enough excuses to send countless other kids into a spiritual tailspin. "But Daniel made up his mind not to eat the food and wine given to them by the king."[14]

Wouldn't it be wonderful to know the joy of our children walking with God when they're gone from our nest? With the example of the Model Parent to guide us and the power of his indwelling Spirit to strengthen us, we can help our children through their formative years and mold them into men and women of God, equipped to do his will.

[13]Genesis 39:7-20
[14]Daniel 1:8, TLB

3

God's Security Blanket

Here we are, faced with the awesome responsibility of molding our children into spiritually dynamic, well-adjusted adults that will bring joy to God's heart and to ours. How are we going to do it? We will try to answer that question throughout this entire book, but one thing stands above all else. It represents what may be our children's greatest need, and the one which parents can fulfill better than anyone else. Children need to be loved by their parents. That's the way God deals with us. "For the Father himself loves you dearly..."[1] "See how very much our heavenly Father loves us..."[2] And that's the way he wants us to deal with our children.

There are many biblical exhortations to love. For example, "Dear friends, let us practice loving each other, for love comes from God and those who are loving and kind show that they are the children of God...."[3] Along with its many other applications, that verse certainly includes love of parent for child. But there are exhortations that are even more specific. The Apostle Paul told

[1] John 16:27, TLB
[2] 1 John 3:1, TLB
[3] 1 John 4:7, TLB

Titus that the older women were to teach the younger women to love their children.[4] And fathers are not excluded from this responsibility in God's order of things. "Like as a father pitieth his children, so the Lord pitieth them that fear him."[5] That word rendered "pitieth" is twice translated "love" in the King James Version.[6] It implies the deepest sort of parental love, tenderness, mercy, and compassion; and it is here attributed to fathers. Mothers and fathers are both to love their children.

Now some are probably asking, "Why should we be reminded of that? Isn't it natural for parents to love their children?" A booming abortion business, recurring instances of child abandonment, and an alarming number of child abuse cases every year would hardly prove it. "That may be the situation with people of the world," the answer comes back, "but we are Christians. We recognize that our children are gifts from God. They are part of us. They are the product of our love for one another. We do love them!" That's true, but do they know it? Do they feel our love all the time, or are there times when they might have good reason to doubt it?

Let me go back to the very beginning as I try to explain what I mean. Every child has the right to be conceived in love, carried with love during those nine months of pregnancy, and warmly welcomed into this world as the prized possession of loving parents. The experts now tell us that an unloving environment during pregnancy may adversely affect a child's later emotional development. After the baby is born, loving surroundings are even more important; he needs to be cuddled, caressed, and cooed. Some babies who have been denied this tender stroking have actually died as a result. Studies have shown that infants may be able to detect a lack of love by harsh tones or careless treatment, much to their emotional distress in later years.

As a child grows older he still needs to be assured over and

4Titus 2:4
5Psalm 103:13, KJV
6Psalm 18:1;
Daniel 1:9

over that he is loved, not for what he does or doesn't do, but just for himself. He needs that assurance with gentle words and with physical closeness. With it he will develop healthy emotional patterns of acceptance and security. Without it, he may become withdrawn, insecure, hostile, or neurotic. Some doctors have discovered that a lack of affection can actually stunt a child's growth. Others have concluded that lack of parental love can cause homosexuality, frigidity, and other aberrations.

A dedicated Christian father told me that his ten-year-old daughter was becoming cold and indifferent toward him. As he evaluated the situation he realized that he was cuddling and carrying her younger brother who was handicapped, but pushing her aside with comments like, "You're a big girl. You can take care of yourself." When he began to demonstrate openly and enthusiastically his love for her, she blossomed into a very warm and loving little girl who enjoyed snuggling up to her daddy. It is our inescapable conclusion, both from the Word of God and from human experience, that a child has the divinely bestowed right to feel secure in his parents' love. It is God's way of getting him started on the road to healthy emotional growth. It is God's security blanket for children.

"But won't our children think they can do anything they want if they feel secure in our love?" That is one of Satan's most subtle lies. He uses it to rob God's children of the joyous security of their heavenly Father's love, and he uses it to rob our children of the satisfying assurance of our love. In both cases, the very opposite is true. Almost all knowledgeable authorities agree that the most potent cause for antisocial behavior, for rebelliousness, disobedience, and discipline problems of all kinds is a lack of affection. Children who know they are loved and accepted, who have no fear of being rejected or abandoned by their parents, do not need to act up to get attention or establish their individual importance and worth. They are important to someone and they know it. They have been accepted, and that assurance brings an inner satisfaction and security. The love they feel from their parents inspires love in their hearts, just as God's love for us inspires us to love.[7] And their love then encourages them to obey us just as our love for God encourages us to obey him.[8] Because they love, they want to please. Rather than inspiring rebellion and disobedience, love restrains it.

After I shared this truth with some parents on one occasion, a kindergarten teacher came to me and told of the most difficult child she had ever encountered in her years of teaching— selfish, belligerent, and hostile toward the other children. The teacher asked God for a genuine love for this child and the ability to help her feel that love. With her new attitudes and actions there was an immediate change, and the child became a cooperative and congenial little student. Camp counselors have told me of problem boys, starved for affection, who respond beautifully when they become aware of someone who really cares for them and shows it. Unfortunately, many of these love-starved children are from Christian homes and are proving to be discipline problems in Bible-believing churches. Maybe we must conclude that the children of Christian parents do not always feel the love God wants them to have. And if that is the case, maybe we should explore some ways of communicating our love so that our children *will* enjoy this essential God-given right.

Just how should our love for our children be expressed? One way is by *words*. Some parents, possibly deprived of love in their own early years, find it impossible to tell their children they love them. They want to, but those tender words will not come out. To force them would seem contrary to their whole makeup and nature. If that is your problem, will you thank God right now for his verbal expressions of love to you in his Word,

[7] 1 John 4:19
[8] 1 John 5:3

and will you ask him to help you tell your children that you love them? You may see an immediate improvement in their behavior.

But words alone won't do it all. Those words must be backed by *actions*. Children are amazingly perceptive. They know when our words are empty and meaningless. "Let us stop just *saying* we love people; let us *really* love them, and *show it* by our *actions*."[9] And by actions I mean more than just feeding them, clothing them, and buying them material things. It is our responsibility to provide for their material needs, but they can sense it when we try to salve our own guilty consciences by giving them gifts to compensate for the love we failed to show.

We need to back our words with *time* spent with them. The Lord does. He is with us always.[10] We really do love our children, but how often we communicate just the opposite with "I don't have time for that now. Go away and leave me alone." We would have more time eventually if we would give them a few minutes of our undivided attention now. That doesn't mean we must drop everything and run every time they want us to do something with them. They can be taught to wait when that is necessary. But for some children, the attention they ask for and wait for never comes. So they develop less acceptable means of getting it, much to their parents' time-consuming embarrassment and dismay. Every time we carelessly push our children aside because they are interrupting something we want to do, we add another scar to their sensitive spirits, and another obstacle to overcome in their growth toward emotional maturity and wholesome adjustment to the world around them.

It isn't just time we're suggesting, however. It's the right kind of time. Quality counts more than quantity. Ten minutes of uninterrupted time spent doing what they want to do may be more valuable than ten hours of distracted time spent scolding, lecturing, or criticizing. Showing interest in the things that

---

[9]1 John 3:18, TLB
[10]Matthew 28:20

interest them will help build a sense of companionship and confidence that will make it easier for them to talk to us in the critical teen years. We must do everything we can to build that confidence, even when our time is limited. My father was a busy pastor. But when I was about six years old he hung a picture of himself and me on his study wall. On it he had written the caption, "Man to man." That was the most valuable treasure in our whole house as far as I was concerned. I remember going into his study when he wasn't there and just staring at it. It made me feel like my dad was my best friend.

Finding time to spend with the children seems to be one of the occupational hazards of the ministry. There have been years in my own ministry when there was so much to do that I felt guilty spending an evening at home with my family. God has helped me reshuffle my priorities according to his master plan. But it can happen to laymen as well. It is possible to get so involved in loving others and doing the Lord's work that we neglect our responsibility to our own children. It is often the pious, super-spiritual, heavenly minded Christians whose children are the greatest discipline problems in the church. Evidently they are so preoccupied with spiritual things that they don't have time to let their children know they love them. The best investment we can ever make is the investment of quality time in our children. The Lord Jesus set a lovely example in this regard. His disciples tried to chase the children away to protect the Savior's time. The Scripture says he was displeased with their attitude. He took the children in his arms and gave them his undivided attention.[11]

Planning for family recreation and fun will help you escape the time trap. And it must be planned. If you are counting on it just happening spontaneously, it probably never will. Dad will have to take a day off periodically and plan to spend it with the family. A successful family night will have to be planned ahead

[11]Mark 10:13-16

of time. A little creative thinking will unveil scores of possible ways to have fun together as a family.

Just for starters, play some games together. We counted sixty-three in our family game closet, accumulated through the years and well-worn with good use. Hobbies can provide togetherness fun. Popping corn, reading books aloud, playing musical instruments together, or just roughhousing on the floor will help to build solid bonds of love. And that's only the beginning. Invest in some backyard athletic equipment like badminton, croquet, horseshoes, or Ping-Pong. Branch out into some other sports that the whole family can enjoy like bowling, tennis, fishing, golf, skating, sledding, skiing, or bicycling. Picnics, weiner roasts, hikes, day trips, and vacations will enlarge your repertoire.

Make mealtime a happy time of sharing. "No grumpiness at the table" is a good rule to follow. Learn to laugh together as a family, even laugh at yourselves. When your children are grown, those times of laughing and silly horseplay will be among their fondest memories of home. Not long ago I talked to a missionary friend who has eight brothers and sisters, all but one of whom are in the Lord's work, and that one was still in school at the time. I asked what his parents did that so influenced their lives. "The one thing that sticks in my mind is the time they spent with us," he said. "Mom sometimes turned down jobs in the church because they would interfere with being a good mother. We all worked for dad in his business, but sometimes he would suggest taking off for awhile in the middle of the day and we would all go out and shoot baskets or play some other game. We had fun together." Times of family fun say, "We love you. We enjoy being with you. You are our most important treasure in this world."

Another way of showing love is by *praise* and *appreciation*. Why is it so easy to scold and criticize our kids when they have done something wrong, but so hard to offer a sincere word of commendation when they have done something good? Every time we let them know that their performance was not quite as good as it might have been, we chip away a little more of their confidence and make them a little more apprehensive about their adequacies and abilities. The most detrimental criticism of all is that which is directed at the personality and character of the child rather than his conduct. We call him clumsy, stupid, bad, ugly, and a host of other unflattering adjectives, and he begins to think of himself in those terms, developing the seeds of an inferiority complex that will cause him grief the rest of his life. Sometimes it is necessary to point out areas of weakness that need to be corrected, but our comments should be directed at what the child *does* rather than who or what he *is*. And we always need to be looking for things he does well, complimenting him for them. That will build in him a sense of confidence and help him overcome the "I can't do anything right" syndrome that could affect most everything he puts his hand to. And it may help convince him that we really do care for him, approve of him, and are glad that he is our child.

We can also help our children feel our love by being *understanding*. Every child is an individual, different from every other child in looks, personality, intelligence, aptitudes, and emotional responses. Each one has the right to be accepted as such and not forced into a mold. Jim may be an eager reader, while Jack is skillful with his hands. Encourage each in his own particular area of interest. It isn't fair to compare one child with another, like "Your sister certainly brought home better grades than this." That kind of comparison not only builds resentment against you for your lack of understanding, but against his sister for causing him this pain of disapproval he is experiencing. Besides, it smacks of favoritism. God's love shows no partiality,[12] and he expects ours to be the same.[13] One

[12]Acts 10:34
[13]James 2:9

of the most tragic commentaries on a home in the Bible was, "Isaac's favorite was Esau, because of the venison he brought home, and Rebekah's favorite was Jacob."[14] The heartache and sorrow which favoritism brought to that home can even be exceeded in ours when one child feels like he is running second in his parents' affections.

In order to help us really understand, we need to listen to what our children are saying. We often jump to conclusions, offer advice, or give lectures without ever hearing our children out. Then we wonder why they stop confiding in us. We need to listen, think, try to understand what they are feeling at the moment, then express words that let them know we understand. Let me illustrate. Suppose your child loses a prized possession such as a brand new baseball. How do you react? "Well, if you had been more careful, you wouldn't have lost it." "You'd lose your head if it weren't screwed on." "When are you going to learn to take care of your things?" "Baseballs don't grow on trees, you know." "Don't gripe at me about it. I didn't lose it." And there may be a hundred other possible retorts designed to convince the child that we really don't care about him, and that a two-dollar baseball is far more important to us than he is. We do need to teach him the value of money and proper care of his belongings. But why not first try something sympathetic like, "And that was your favorite ball, wasn't it?" Or something helpful like, "C'mon, we'll look for it together. Where do you think you had it last?" Or something encouraging like, "Maybe we'll find it when we clean out the garage." Then you will convince him that you really care for him, that you are his friend rather than his antagonist and critic.

We express love to our children by respecting them too. They are persons whom God has made with value and eternal worth, and they should be treated accordingly. That means we should

---

[14]Genesis 25:28, TLB

never laugh at their weaknesses or ridicule their idiosyn-
crasies. "George, you throw a ball like a girl." "Well, how's my
little butterball Becky today?" "Just innocent fun," we say, but
it damages their sensitive spirits, destroys their fragile self-
image, and puts another strain on their struggle to maturity.
Respect also means we should not talk about them disparag-
ingly in their presence like they were fixtures in the room.
Messages that unwittingly enter those little ears may be permanently inscribed on their souls, misdirecting their lives for
many years to come. Dad says, "I'm afraid Jack never will
amount to anything." If Jack hears him say that often enough,
he will soon become convinced that it's true. And he probably
won't amount to anything. There is not much reason for him to
try. His dad, who knows much more than he does, has already
concluded that he is not capable of accomplishing anything
worthwhile in life.

Love will be communicated by our *tone of voice* likewise.
You may say you love your children, but they are not feeling
love when you scream, "Stop that this instant," or whine, "You
kids are getting on my nerves today." Sometimes we need to be
reminded that children are people who have the right to be
talked to kindly and pleasantly just as we would talk to any
other person we cared for. Anger is never a valid expression of
love. Love "… is not irritable or touchy."[15] Maybe we ought to
evaluate our own anger index when our children respond to us
with hostility.

"But they can be so exasperating and irritating." Yes, and we
need to admit that our love is not enough, that it wears thin and
finally explodes. Then we need to yield our wills to Christ and
let his Spirit express his love through us. The natural product
of that Spirit-filled life will be God's kind of love.[16] Then we
will be able to communicate our love to our children even
when they are acting like children. And they will be able to

[15]1 Corinthians 13:5, TLB
[16]Galatians 5:22

relax in our love and get down to the business of growing up instead of expending their energies trying to get our attention or establish their importance by one unacceptable means after another. And we will begin to experience the joy God intended us to have in our children.

4
Do as I Do

Why do some kids raised in Christian homes really turn on to Jesus Christ, get vitally involved in living for him, growing in him, and sharing him with others, while other kids in the same environment seem to drop out spiritually during their teen years? The whole church routine becomes a drag to them and they couldn't care less about the things of the Lord. This is a complicated question which Christian leaders have been grappling with for years. There are certainly many factors involved with different problems contributing to each individual case. No single answer will suffice for all. But one thing keeps coming up in both my contact with Christian families and my discussions with youth leaders, and I cannot escape the importance of it. That is the truth revealed in Galatians 6:7, 8: "Don't be misled; remember that you can't ignore God and get away with it: a man will always reap just the kind of crop he sows! If he sows to please his own desires, he will be planting seeds of evil and he will surely reap a harvest of spiritual decay and death; but if he plants the good things of the Spirit, he will reap the everlasting life which the Holy Spirit gives him" (TLB).

Reaping what we sow applies to many areas of life, but among them will inevitably be our relationship with our children. We are going to reap just the kind of crop we sow in them. And unfortunately for us, what we sow in them involves not only how we treat them or what we say to them, but how we *act* before them. In other words, we cannot expect our children to excel us in spiritual stature or to be what we ourselves are not. It is our responsibility to set an example before them of all we want them to be.

This is the way the Model Parent deals with us. When he tells us what we ought to be, he sets the standard by his own example. "But be holy now in everything you do, just as the Lord is holy, who invited you to be his child. He himself has said, 'You must be holy, for I am holy.' "[1] His own perfect holiness gives him the right to require the same of us. We would be quite put out if he demanded more than he himself demonstrated. But instead, he sets a perfect pattern for us to follow. The Lord Jesus used this same approach with his disciples. "I have given you an example to follow: do as I have done to you."[2] He set such a high standard because he knew we could not be expected to rise above the level he established. "How true it is that a servant is not greater than his master."[3] If we are to deal with our children as the Lord deals with us, we must set a high example of all we want them to be.

A poor example before our children will have its effect on generations to come. The Lord is merciful and forgiving, but he warns that children will feel the impact of their parents' sins to the third and fourth generations.[4] Does that mean that God puts a curse on three or four generations, or that something is passed on by heredity that hexes them? I don't think so. But sin creates a certain kind of environment in the home, psychologically and

[1] 1 Peter 1:15, 16, TLB
[2] John 13:15, TLB
[3] John 13:16a, TLB
[4] Numbers 14:18

spiritually, an environment that makes its contribution to the character of our children. When they marry, they will probably create the same home environment they experienced as they were growing up and perpetuate the sins and shortcomings they saw in us, with many of the same unhappy consequences.

Actually, the home they establish may be worse than ours. I can think of some professing Christian homes where the parents fussed and fought a good deal of the time. There was little Christ-like love shown to the children. The Lord Jesus was not allowed to play a very prominent role in their home life and the things of Christ were seldom discussed, except to criticize other Christians. But in front of their Christian friends, the parents were careful to maintain the "good Christian" facade. Their children saw through the hypocrisy of it all, decided it wasn't for them, repudiated Christianity, and established a secular home when they married. I wonder how many generations will be affected by the parents' sin? God says at least three or four. And there is no guarantee that even then someone will come to know Christ and reverse the trend. If it happens, it will be entirely of God's grace.

It's time to halt that kind of downward spiral, time to yield ourselves to the control of the Holy Spirit and become what God wants us to be, time to begin setting a Christ-like example before our children and repair any damage that may have already been done. The prophet Isaiah called on the people of his day to get their hearts right with God. He made this beautiful promise to them if they would: "And they that shall be of thee shall build the old waste places; thou shalt raise up the foundations of many generations; and thou shalt be called, The repairer of the breach, The restorer of paths to dwell in."[5] He was referring primarily to rebuilding the walls and streets of Jerusalem, but we cannot miss the spiritual application. If believing parents will submit themselves to God and do his will,

[5]Isaiah 58:12, KJV

they and their children will be able to repair the ruins of many generations and acquire the enviable titles, "The repairer of the breach," and "The restorer of paths to dwell in."

We can help put an end to the decline of the Christian home. Our homes can be different. God isn't going to accept time-worn excuses like, "But that's the way I was raised," or "That's the way my father and mother treated me." If what we are doing is wrong, we need to change it. When we turn to the Lord in submission and trust, he will help us mend what is torn apart and restore the right way to live. Generations to come will thank us for it.

There are some hackneyed old sayings that few of us have been able to escape through the years: One is, "Actions speak louder than words"; another, "What you do speaks so loud, I can't hear what you say." They aren't found in the Bible, but the idea they promulgate is far more biblical than we might imagine. The Apostle Paul suggested to some of his friends, "And you should follow my example, just as I follow Christ's."[6] To others he said, "Keep putting into practice all you learned from me and saw me doing, and the God of peace will be with you."[7] I wonder if we could say that to our children. Another well-worn saying may better reflect our normal approach, "Do as I say, not as I do." Satan must have inspired that one, and if we continue to use it, we can count on our children becoming more and more rebellious.

To a young pastor, Paul wrote, "... in speech, conduct, love, faith and purity, show yourself an example of those who believe."[8] He knew Timothy's congregation wouldn't listen to him very long if they didn't see in his own life some evidence that he was practicing what he preached. The same principle relates to parents and children. We should be able to say, "Do as I say, *and* as I do." And the kids will be able to spot in a minute the phoniness of anything less.

[6] 1 Corinthians 11:1, TLB
[7] Philippians 4:9, TLB
[8] 1 Timothy 4:12, NASB

For example, we want our children to be kind. We teach them to speak kindly to other people and about other people. But they may hear us tear a friend to shreds verbally, or hear us speak most unkindly to each other or even to them. They will probably do as we do rather than as we say. We teach our children to be honest. But when we're all waiting in line to buy tickets to some interesting attraction, we may say, "Tell them you're only eleven." Or they may hear us discussing how we successfully padded our expense account or faked our way out of a traffic ticket when we knew we had broken the law. And we'll have nobody to blame but ourselves when we catch them lying or cheating.

We teach them not to steal. But we gloated just a bit because the clerk at the market overchanged us, and we didn't return the money to its rightful owner. And our children begin to believe that it's alright to steal a dollar here or there under certain conditions.

We want our children to learn that whining and fussing do not get them what they want. Yet we sometimes whine and fuss at them when they don't please us, and we may whine and fuss at each other when things don't go our way. So they will just keep on whining and fussing their way through their childhood and youth years. And they'll do it when they get married, and who knows how many people ultimately will feel the misery of our poor example?

The illustrations can be multiplied many times over. We teach them that God will take care of their needs, that worry has no place in the life of a Christian. Yet we may worry ourselves sick over our latest little problem and pop our tranquilizers with addictive zeal when the pressure's on. We try to teach them to listen to us when we speak. But we're often too busy to pay any attention to what they are saying. Sometimes we're shouting at them when we tell them to lower their voices, or nagging them to pick up their things when ours are strewn all over the house. One woman told me that her parents washed her mouth out with soap for saying "golly" or "gee" when she was little. But she heard them through the bedroom wall swearing at each other. As you might well imagine, her emotional problems were immense.

We want our children to keep their word, but our promises to them mean very little if something comes up we would rather do. We encourage them not to be materialistic, yet they hear us complaining about the small house, the run-down car or the styleless clothes. We tell them to walk with the Lord, but they see no evidence that we are spending time in the Word or in prayer. We teach them how important it is to be with the Lord's people on his day for instruction and worship. Yet we stay home for trivial reasons, or maybe even take them hiking or fishing during services. As Bible-believing Christians we want them to be concerned about the needs of a lost world, but we seldom mention any missionaries or pray for them as a family.

If we want our children to be what God wants them to be, then we must show them the way. Our failure in this respect is sad enough, but there is something even sadder, and that is our unwillingness to admit it. Too often we insist that there is nothing really wrong with the way we are living or the example we are setting. And this basic dishonesty about ourselves becomes our undoing. Children can see through the sham and hypocrisy of it all, and it destroys them.

Maybe we can label the basic problem "rut Christianity." Rut Christians may be true believers in a state of spiritual immaturity or they may only know Christian vocabulary rather than knowing Christ himself. The jargon differs from church to church, but it doesn't take long to pick up the "in" terms. In either case, they carefully maintain the routine, religious habit pattern that is expected of them. They attend church fairly regularly—maybe not as often as they should, but often enough to maintain the proper image. They give their money to the church—maybe not as much as they could, but enough to convince folks they're genuinely committed to Christ. They may even accept some responsibilities in the church; after all, church work *is* important. But they systematically and skillfully mask their faults, sins, shortcomings, doubts, inner struggles, temptations, weaknesses, tensions, and conflicts, lest they destroy the "good Christian" image they want to project. They have never really enjoyed the personal presence of the living Christ, nor do they let him control every detail of their lives. He's a Sunday-only Savior, but they try their hardest to make folks think he's real to them.

They may have an angry shouting match all the way to church. But as soon as they step out of the car they put on their friendly Sunday smiles and greet folks with their saintly Sunday voices. And the kids begin to think, "It isn't real. The Lord isn't real. He doesn't make any difference in the way we live. It's all a big game." Then they may see a certain unhappiness in their parents' daily lives, a dull, zestless, dissatisfying routine all week long—work, eat, read the paper, putter around in the yard, watch TV, go to bed, over and over, day after day. And Jesus Christ is no part of it at all. They sense that their folks are plodding along through life pretty much because they're stuck with it. They hear about the joy and peace and purpose that Jesus brings; they may even hear their parents give a testimony to that effect in church. But they know better. They see them where they live.

So the kids often do one of two things—they either throw over the whole thing, openly rebel and repudiate Christianity, or they fall into the same empty, powerless "rut Christianity" their parents practiced. A few may fall in love with Jesus Christ and become *real!* Thank God for them. But they're probably in the minority. Some people say, "Why doesn't the church do something about the situation? Why doesn't the church show them that Christ is real, that he can make a difference in the way people live?" Maybe we should be reminded that the pastors, youth leaders, teachers, and workers in our church are the mothers and fathers from our homes. Our churches can be no more vital than our homes are.

What is the answer? Some will be tempted to say, "Well, I'll be honest then. I'll throw all my good habits to the wind, stay out of church when I feel like it, broadcast my sins for all to see, and let everybody know the Lord isn't real to me." I know folks who have just about done that, but it didn't solve a thing. In fact, it only complicated their problems and caused greater rebellion in their children. There are at least four things that will help us:

1. *Get to know Jesus Christ intimately.* That is going to take time in the Word and time in prayer. But we must do it! Our Christian lives will never be more than a rut unless Jesus Christ becomes our devoted friend, unless our aim in life is to know him warmly and well, just as it was for Paul.[9]

2. *Let Jesus Christ make us what he wants us to be.* Then we won't have to pretend anymore or calculate ways to make people think we're spiritual giants. We will be men and women of God in all genuine humility. We must begin by yielding ourselves to Jesus Christ, then continue by consciously depending on him every minute to help us be what we should be. There is really no other way to change significantly. We can turn over new leaves and make new resolutions until we're fed up with our failures. But when we commit our lives to Jesus Christ, he helps us make the necessary changes.

3. *Let Jesus Christ become involved in every detail of our lives.* This is what we want to teach our children to do (see the next chapter) but we must do it ourselves first. Christ is in-

9Philippians 3:10

terested in every particular of our lives, and we need to share everything with him. He wants us to acknowledge his presence all the time, seek his wisdom in every decision, talk to him about even the smallest matters, and make him a regular part of our daily conversation. The result will be some exciting answers to prayer and some thrilling evidences of divine guidance that we can use to show our children just how wonderful the Lord is.

4. *Be honest about our faults.* We have an old sin nature, and there are times when it gains control of our lives. We may lose our temper with our children or be cranky and irritable with them. Don't be afraid to admit it. If we've acted in a self-centered, unchristlike manner, then we owe them an apology. The command to confess our faults one to another doesn't exclude children from those who deserve our apologies.[10] Some people protest, "But it will destroy their confidence in me." No it won't. They already know we've sinned. Refusing to admit it is the thing that destroys the confidence. Acknowledging our wrongs will build confidence and respect and draw us closer together.

I can remember heatedly scolding one of my boys for something he had done, only to realize later that I had grossly overreacted. When I told him I had behaved badly, he put his arm on my shoulder and said, "That's okay, Dad. Nobody's perfect." I knew that already, but the experience left an aftermath of close companionship. There have been other occasions like that with my children, but far fewer than there should have been.

Admitting our faults also encourages our children to be honest about theirs, instead of pretending they don't exist and perpetuating the same old "rut Christianity." And this is what we are praying for and working toward, isn't it? May God help us to unmask our hearts before him, then honestly and openly

[10]James 5:16

acknowledge our wrongs to one another. It will open new avenues of communication with our children and establish strong ties that Satan will not be able to break.

One note of warning must be sounded before we leave this subject. A poor parental example is not the only reason for children going astray. There are many other factors, not the least of which is the child's own determined self-will. We need to be very careful about condemning the parents of rebellious children. Rather than our critical glances and chilling avoidance, they need our loving friendship, sympathetic support, and faithful prayers.

5
Precept upon Precept

Our goal as Christian parents is to produce
spiritually mature adults, ready to serve the Lord
in any way he directs. We work toward that goal
by loving our children as God loves us and by
setting a Christ-like example for them to follow.
But even then we've only begun. The next step is
urgent, and may best be introduced by these instructions to Timothy: "But as for you, continue
in what you have learned and have become convinced of, because you know those from whom
you learned it, and how from infancy you have
known the holy Scriptures, which are able to
make you wise for salvation through faith in
Christ. All Scripture is God-breathed and is useful
for teaching, rebuking, correcting and training in
righteousness, so that the man of God may be
thoroughly equipped for every good work."[1]

That last statement describes the very person
we want to produce—a man of God thoroughly
equipped for every good work. How can a child be
brought to that place? According to this passage,
it is by building the Word of God into his life from

his very earliest days. If we want our children to turn out as God wants them to be, we must teach them the Scriptures. Our heavenly Father encourages his children to feed on his Word.[2] And human parents who know him will do the same for their children.

We have decried the removal of the Bible from our public schools, but God never gave the public school system the responsibility of instilling his Word into the hearts and lives of our children. He committed it to us, their parents. That principle was established very early in God's dealings with his ancient people Israel and has never been superseded. "O Israel, listen: Jehovah is our God, Jehovah alone. You must love him with *all* your heart, soul, and might. And you must think constantly about these commandments I am giving you today. You must teach them to your children and talk about them when you are at home or out for a walk; at bedtime and the first thing in the morning."[3]

Unfortunately, the Bible is a closed book from one Sunday to the next in many Christian homes. Parents have evidently decided to let the Sunday school and church handle the job of making the Scriptures a vital part of their children's lives. But the Sunday school and church only have the children for two or three hours out of the 168 in a week. Even if our teachers were the most skilled people on earth at relating the principles of God's Word to the lives of our children, that amount of time is negligible compared to the time other influences mold their lives. If we want our children to be spiritually mature and fully equipped to serve Jesus Christ, we will need to supplement that scant diet of Bible teaching with some consistent instruction in the home. While some may avoid this responsibility by insisting we are not under law, the New Testament exhortation to fathers to raise their children in the instruction of the Lord would indicate that the principle has never been outdated.[4]

[2]1 Peter 2:2
[3]Deuteronomy 6:4-7, TLB
[4]Ephesians 6:4

It seems as though parents are concerned about almost everything except this most important element of their children's
training. They spend a great deal of money to clothe them in
style; after all, they don't want them to look different from their
friends. They try to provide the very best of food and shelter,
and many of us have more of both than we really need. No cost
is too great to correct any physical handicaps—crooked teeth,
greasy skin, or pigeon toes. They take great pains to see that
their secular education is the very best available. But they neglect the one thing that can make their children men and women
of God, that is, an experiential knowledge of his inspired Word.
It is no surprise that many Christian young people lack an
interest in spiritual matters and lack the strength to resist the
great temptations of our times. It is understandable that so few
enter the Lord's work and some turn their backs on him completely.

Why are we so careless in this matter? A clue may be found
right here in this central Old Testament passage. "And you
must think constantly about these commandments I am giving
you today."[5] The Word must occupy a prominent place in our
own hearts and minds before we can impart it to our children.
We cannot teach them what we do not possess ourselves, what
we have not made a part of our own experience. We cannot
show them how the Word relates to their problems, their decisions, their motives, their goals, and their behavior if we have
never learned to relate it to our own. Setting an example before
our children begins right here with our relationship to the Lord
and his Word.

How relevant is Jesus Christ to your daily life? How faithful
are you in applying the principles of his Word to everyday
living? We must get into the Word for ourselves, let it saturate
our minds and regulate our life-style. Then alone will we be
qualified to move on to the next verse and teach it to our chil-

---

[5]Deuteronomy 6:6

dren. The question is, "Are you ready to move on?" Decide to make the Bible the dominant guiding force in your life. Ask God to give you the kind of hunger for his Word that draws you away from less important things which make no worthwhile contribution to your life. Then you will be ready to make that Word a vital part of your child's life.

Where then do we begin? One small but helpful part of implanting the Word involves setting time aside for the family to gather together and talk about its living truths. We sometimes call it family worship. This may be family worship here in Deuteronomy 6:7: "You must teach them to your children and talk about them when you are at home ..." (TLB). We can picture the Jewish family seated together at home, sharing the great doctrines which God had revealed to them through Moses, rehearsing God's great faithfulness to them through the years and reminding each other of their responsibilities to him.

"Oh, but we don't have time for that at our house." One survey exposed the distressing fact that less than fifteen percent of our evangelical Christian homes have family worship with any degree of regularity. Maybe you are part of the eighty-five percent who neglect it and your excuse has been lack of time. That seems to be the most popular one. But most of us have time to do the things we want to do. What we need to do is move family worship up on our priority list. Maybe your excuse has been the difficulty of getting every member of the family together at the same time and in the same place. In some houses, everyone leaves at a different hour in the morning, so each one grabs his breakfast on the run. Everyone is still running in opposite directions after dinner in the evening. Johnny has Little League, Betty has band, Dad has a board meeting, and Mother goes to the missionary circle. There just isn't any time when everybody can get together at once.

If that's the case at your house, maybe it's time to reevaluate your way of living. It is possible for family members to become too busy for their own good. There will inevitably be days when some activity interferes with family worship. That is nothing to fee guilty about. And the time to have it will obviously vary from family to family. Some will be able to get together around the breakfast table. For others, after supper will provide the right opportunity. Bedtime may be the only live option for a few. The point is, find a suitable time and, generally speaking, abide by it.

It is possible that some have not tried family worship because they don't know what to do. Maybe we can offer a few suggestions. All of these elements need not necessarily be present every time you gather together, but here are some possibilities:

1. *Bible reading.* Remember to make it understandable to the children present. There is nothing magical about hearing the words of the Scripture if they are not understood. Use modern translations at times. Read passages that are most helpful to your daily lives. While all of the Bible is inspired of God and profitable, some parts are more applicable to the needs of daily living than others. The genealogies of 1 Chronicles 1-11, for example, would not be very conducive to family worship.

It would be helpful to memorize a pertinent verse each week, or memorize an extended passage over a period of time. Be sure to explain the meaning of the passage and apply it to the members of the family circle. Talk about how it applies to your own life and what changes you need to make as a result of hearing God's Word. That will encourage the rest of the family to do the same. Some families act out the narrative portions of the Scripture to help fix the facts in their children's minds. All this may take some preparation. While some may recoil in horror at such a thought, we are talking about the most important issues of life, and no cost should be too great to see that our children grow in their knowledge of the Lord through his Word.

2. *Prayer.* Make prayer meaningful to the children present. There is no need for long involved prayers, particularly where small children are concerned. Talk to God as a personal friend who is concerned about the specific things familiar to those in the family circle. Talk to him about problems the children are having, missionaries they know, their relatives, pastors, teachers, and friends, especially friends who need to know the Lord. Then be sure to discuss at future sessions how God has answered your prayers.

3. *Other literature.* Variety is the key to an interesting and captivating family worship. You can use a Bible storybook, books of Bible doctrine for children, or storybooks that use modern life situations to teach Bible truths and their application. Your local Christian bookstore will have a selection to choose from. You could set one day a week aside for a continuing Christian fiction story or a missionary biography. Read missionary letters periodically to acquaint children with the needs of the world. On Sundays you can talk about the application of the pastor's message to your lives. There may be days when you merely want to share the biblical significance of a newspaper or magazine article. Keep it varied and your children will look forward to it.

4. *Music.* Some families like to sing together. That may be catastrophic for others. But if you can do it, singing some of the great hymns of the church or choruses with a Bible-centered message will be a meaningful worship experience. Music has a way of inscribing a message on the soul for keeps, so make sure the message is biblically sound. Even if you are not much on vocalizing, you can fill your home with good recorded Christian music, creating a spiritual atmosphere and implanting eternal spiritual truths in your children's hearts.

In addition to these four elements of family worship, here are a few other suggestions to help make family worship pleasant rather than painful. For one thing, *keep it relaxed and informal*. Avoid the stiff, strained compulsive atmosphere that makes some children dread it like the plague. If it's fun, your children will look back on it as one of the highlights of their life at home. If it's tedious, it could wreck their walk with God. I was counseling Stan and Sally regarding some problems in their marriage and I sensed that the underlying cause was spiritual. A question or two brought this startling statement from Stan. "Yeah, we had family worship at our house. My dad got his Bible out, told everybody to shut up, then droned through a chapter or two in a pious tone before he went back to fighting with mom. I hated every minute of it." Family worship should be a "want to," not a "have to." It would be better to have an exciting and enjoyable experience once a week than a boring and irrelevant one every day.

Fun does not mean frivolity, however. *Keep it reverent.* This is a time to talk about spiritual matters, and anything extraneous to that is out of order. Sometimes children develop an uncanny ability to sabotage family worship. If they aren't in the mood for it, they can become silly and giddy and destroy it for everyone else. A firm hand will be necessary on those occasions.

Particularly for the sake of the younger members, *keep it brief*—not rushed, but purposely planned to be short. Five to ten minutes is long enough unless a spontaneous discussion ensues in which the children are vitally interested and involved. That has happened periodically at our house, and what a blessing it has been. My oldest son recently told me that "those famous Strauss family discussions" were one of the things he remembers most fondly about his childhood.

If a wide age span exists between the children in a family, it might be advantageous to gear the point of emphasis to a different aged child on successive days. As far as leadership is concerned, the biblical pattern puts that responsibility upon dad.[6] If he is an unbeliever or a carnal Christian who refuses to take the lead, mother should do it. But in either case, get started now. Every Christian family needs to gather together around the Word.

Ten minutes of family worship should not be the extent of the family's training in the Word, however. We need to avail ourselves of every possible opportunity to show our children how the Word of God applies to their lives, such as when we are "... out for a walk; at bedtime and first thing in the morning."[7] Jesus Christ is interested in every detail of our lives and his Word affects every facet of living. We need to let him become involved in every part of our family's life. Take even the smallest problems to him in prayer as a family, anytime, anywhere, things as small as a lost pocketknife or a poor grade in a pop quiz. Thank him for the answers, whatever they are. Acknowledge his kindness together during times of family fun. Seek his wisdom and grace together during times of family crisis. Relate God's Word to experiences the children have had, situations at hand, television programs they have seen, community affairs and news events with which they are familiar. Make the Lord himself the most common topic of conversation in your home. Give the children good Christian literature to read and good Christian music to listen to. Weave the Lord and his Word into the fabric of their lives.

Some may be wondering at what age the children should be when we begin this intensive program of Bible training. The prophet Isaiah may be of help on that question. "Whom shall he teach knowledge? And whom shall he make to understand doctrine? them that are weaned from the milk, and drawn from the breasts. For precept must be upon precept, precept upon precept; line upon line, line upon line; here a little, and there a little."[8] That seems to be rather young, doesn't it? Timothy's

[6]Ephesians 6:4
[7]Deuteronomy 6:7, TLB
[8]Isaiah 28:9, 10, KJV

experience of learning the Scriptures from infancy would confirm the prophet's intent. God wants us to make his Word a part of our children's lives from their earliest conscious moments. The simplest truths come first; then as their minds mature, the more difficult doctrines follow. Precept upon precept, line upon line, here a little and there a little, the very mind of God unfolds before them.

What will be the result of teaching our children the Scriptures? For one thing, they will trust the Lord Jesus Christ as their personal Savior. The Scriptures make one wise unto salvation.[9] "For you have been born again, not of perishable seed, but of imperishable, through the living and enduring word of God."[10] The Spirit of God uses the Word of God to create a sense of guilt over sin and the need to trust the substitutionary death of Jesus Christ. That trust brings salvation.[11]

There are two extremes to avoid when it comes to the salvation of our children. One danger is saying little or nothing to them about receiving Christ as their Savior. Some Christian parents have the erroneous idea that their children are saved because they are. Since they themselves are God's children, they seem to think their children automatically become God's grandchildren. So they neglect to teach them the reality and awfulness of sin, and the need for personal trust in Christ. As a result, the children grow up without ever being confronted with the necessity for a personal decision. They may live and die without Christ simply because their parents assumed they were Christians. Other parents avoid the issue because they don't want to force anything on their children. "We're going to let them decide for themselves," they affirm. That may sound very noble, but heaven and hell are at stake here. The children must make their own decision, but we must guide them with the Word.

There is a second extreme to beware, and that is pushing a

[9]2 Timothy 3:15
[10]1 Peter 1:23, NIV
[11]Acts 16:31

child to take some action like inviting Jesus into his heart before he comprehends the real issues of sin and the substitutionary death of Christ. Children respond easily to attractive offers. What child doesn't want Jesus in his life? What child doesn't want to escape hell and go to heaven? Then again, a child may make a decision to get the approval of an adult, or to get an award such as a Bible, or simply because his friends are doing it. Genuine salvation comes through the convicting work of the Holy Spirit, and that is not always coincident with the alluring appeals or frightening warnings of misguided adults.

That is not to say a very young child cannot be saved. I would not venture to set limits on the Holy Spirit, and some children are able to grasp the issues long before others. I know children who have trusted Christ as Savior at three years of age and the change in their lives indicated that it was real. The important thing is that the child understand the seriousness of his sin and his inability to save himself, then intelligently put his trust in the all-sufficiency of Christ's sacrifice. Teaching him the Word of God precept upon precept will bring about that understanding. When the Holy Spirit has done his work through the Word, we'll know it by the child's open and spontaneous response and his wholehearted commitment to the Savior. Then he will be genuinely born again and his life will be changed. Sometimes young teens who have made decisions very early in life begin to doubt their salvation and want to be sure. Encourage them to settle it and claim the assurance of the Scripture from that day forward.[12] It is possible in some cases that their early experience was analogous to a premature birth and needs to be reaffirmed.

Salvation is only the beginning, however. After a child has been born again, we can expect fruit in his life as with any other believer.[13] So we keep teaching him the Word to help him grow into a productive Christian. "Like newborn babies, long

[12]e.g. 1 John 5:11-13
[13]2 Corinthians 5:17

for the pure milk of the word, that by it you may grow in respect to salvation."[14] That is God's way of bringing believers to spiritual maturity and strength. Faithfully building the Word of God into the lives of our children may help solve some of the discipline problems in our Sunday schools. It may reduce some of the rebelliousness among our youth. It may prevent some of the matrimonial crack-ups we see among professing Christians. It may eliminate some of the personnel shortages in the worldwide ministry of the gospel. And it may check some of the shipwrecks among full-time Christian servants.

I talked recently with two leaders in one of our nation's outstanding youth movements. They shared with me some of the tragic stories of staff dropouts suffered by their organization. In most cases these young Christian workers had not had the benefit of childhood training in the Word, and as a result they wore not capable of coping with the mammoth obstacles Satan had thrown in their way. God can radically change a person and transform him into a profitable servant of Jesus Christ at any point in his life. But there is no substitute for systematically learning the truths of the Scripture from one's earliest days. It builds solid, stable men and women of God who bring joy to our hearts.

[14]1 Peter 2:2, NASB

6
Growing Hedges
by the Way

One disturbing fact becomes apparent all too quickly as we seek to follow God's perfect example of parenthood—we have a sinful nature that God doesn't have. Although we want to love our children as God loves, set them a good example as God does, and patiently implant his Word into their lives as he desires, they keep doing things that bother us and we respond all too humanly.

When they are careless or disorderly, we react with irritation because of the extra work they cause us. Whether it was muddy shoes, spilled milk, or any one of a hundred other annoyances, every parent has experienced moments of angry exasperation with his youngsters. When they are disrespectful and disobedient, we sometimes retort with a heated tirade because our authority and self-esteem are threatened. When they are unmannerly before our friends, we scold them indignantly because our reputations are at stake. We know our actions are unloving and selfish, damaging to the children, and deadening to the warm affection and happy atmosphere we want to pervade our homes. But we cannot seem to help ourselves.

We may subconsciously try to prove our love by compensating for our unloving actions. Some parents become *overindulgent.* They give their child practically everything he wants. He becomes lazy, irresponsible, and ungrateful, harboring the strange notion that the world owes him everything while he has no obligation to anyone. That certainly isn't love.

Other parents become *overprotective.* They shield their child from every unpleasant problem and difficult decision in life. They may even try to protect him from the consequences of his own irresponsible behavior by refusing to consider what teachers and friends are telling them about him, or by defending him when he has done wrong and trying to get him off easy. Their child's behavior is a poor reflection on them, and if they have never been honest about themselves, they find it hard to face their child's faults. Overprotectiveness is a cruel imitation for love that leaves a child ill-prepared to cope with the realities of life.

Still others become *overpermissive,* letting the child do almost anything he pleases even if it encroaches on the rights of others. So he becomes undisciplined, inconsiderate, and belligerent, making life unpleasant for nearly everyone whose life he touches. Overpermissiveness is not love. In fact, it is the very opposite of love as we shall see from God's Word.

While God's love for us is unlimited in scope,[1] it nevertheless sets limits on our conduct. After teaching us that our love for God grows out of his love for us, the Apostle John writes, "For this is the love of God, that we keep his commandments."[2] The love relationship between our heavenly Father and us compels him to set bounds for our behavior. He knows what is best for us, and in gracious lovingkindness he requires us to comply.

[1]Ephesians 3:17-19
[2]1 John 5:3, KJV

If this is the way God deals with his children, then we must follow his example. Our love for our children will not permit them unrestrained expression of every whim. Love sets limits. These limits seem to be the major point of Proverbs 22:6, one of the most famous verses in the Bible on child-rearing: "Train up a child in the way he should go: and when he is old, he will not depart from it" (KJV).

Much has been written about this verse and not all expositors agree on its meaning. While the verb translated "train" is most often rendered "dedicate" in the Old Testament, its primary and literal meaning is "to press in, to make narrow." In other words, God says we are to narrow our children in, hedge them in to the way he wants them to go. Children do not always know what the right path is, so we grow hedges—thick, tall hedges on both sides of the path—that limit them, close them in to the right way. If we do this properly through their early years, they will grow to be well-adjusted, self-disciplined adults. When we lived in Fort Worth, Texas, we visited the botanical gardens where there was a maze of winding paths lined in with thick hedges. If we stayed between the hedges we always came out at the right place eventually. Just so, God wants us to hedge our children in so that they will turn out right.

"In the way he should go" means literally "upon the mouth of his way." It projects the image of a flock or herd passing through a narrow gateway. Some say it means "according to his way," that is, in accord with the mental and emotional capacity of the child at each stage of his development, or consistent with his own peculiar characteristics. While the phrase could possibly mean "according to his way," that meaning in this case would leave the last half of the verse without any sense. From what specific thing, then, would he not depart when he becomes an adult? We certainly do not want him to maintain any lower level of mental or emotional maturity, or hold on to any unacceptable characteristics. We want him to grow. But the verse says that the path we establish for him as a child is the very same path he will follow when he is old. "The way he should go" refers rather to the way God wants him to live. It is our responsibility to regulate his behavior while he is young so he will learn habit patterns of self-discipline and submission to authority. When he is old he will be able to maintain that self-discipline and submit himself to the authority of God.

Small children are not able to regulate their own behavior properly. They simply do not have sufficient experience to know what is best for them. For example, Tommy Toddler doesn't know what will bring him pain or bodily injury, so we set limits for him. We do not allow him to put his hand into the toaster. He might learn something about the use of a toaster that way, but he will also permanently disfigure his hand. So we insist that he obey us. We teach him, train him, hedge him in to the right way, refuse to let him deviate from it. Our love keeps him from checking out that shiny chrome appliance with the glowing red innards.

Our love will also keep him from learning behavior patterns that will bring him unhappiness later in life. For example, we know that whining and fussing to get his own way will bring grief to his relationships with other people. So our love refuses to let him get his own way by selfishly demanding it. Even very young children who have been raised properly understand this principle. A little girl was driving her mother to distraction with a tantrum in the aisle of a supermarket, screaming and crying, demanding one thing after another. Little Brenda, looking at the spectacle rather disgustedly, turned to her mother and said, "Mommy, that lady wouldn't let her little girl act that way if she loved her."

If the early training has been adequate, we will be able to

permit our children more freedom and allow them to make more decisions as they grow older. But love still sets limits. It's usually easier to say "yes" to a teenager than "no." But love may demand some "noes," and love is willing to bear the possible unpleasant consequences of a "no" if the long-range benefit warrants it.

The world has grossly misinterpreted the meaning of love with its permissive child psychology of unrestrained expressionism. God's love sets limits, and the advantages of his method are obvious. For one thing, God's way gives children a sense of security. Put a child in a familiar fenced yard with some toys to play with and he'll feel secure even with cars speeding nearby. But put him out by himself in a big city with the freedom to roam anywhere he pleases, and his security will turn to sheer terror. Children want boundaries, even if they do not fully understand their feelings. Their sinful natures cry for freedom to do as they please. But they are confused and disturbed when they get away with more than they know they should. Uncontrolled children are seldom happy. They feel unloved and insecure.

Teens are very little different in this regard. Most of them grumble about the restrictions their parents make, but many a young rebel with unhindered liberty to do as he pleases has openly admitted, "I wish my folks cared enough about me to make some rules and stick with them." Other kids who have run off and gotten married to escape their parents' restrictions have found themselves longing for the security of home. Young people sometimes disobey to test their parents' love, to see if their folks care enough to restrict them. Even in their moments of rebellion, they cannot understand why their parents let them act as they do if they really love them.

Another benefit of God's way relates to the matter of authority. God wants Christians to be submissive to governmental authority.[3] But a submissive spirit is learned in the home by willing submission to parents' authority. A child who gets his own way continually at home will eventually face a world where he cannot have his own way, where laws restrict his behavior to protect the rights of others. If he insists on his own way there, he brings upon himself multiplied misery and heartache. Most of those who openly rebel against governmental authority were never taught obedience in the home.

More important still, God wants us to be submissive to his authority.[4] One reason many young people resist God's Word and God's will for their lives is that they were never taught submission to the word and will of their parents. Obedience to parents is obedience to the Lord. "Children, obey your parents; this is the right thing to do because God has placed them in authority over you."[5]

Establishing limits has other profitable effects. It removes a great burden from both the child and the parent. Some kids are confused because they don't know what is expected of them. Certain behavior may be accepted one day but it makes parental sparks fly the next, and the kids don't know what to think. It's a relief for them to know specifically what the rules are. I questioned thirty-five college students recently to learn their thoughts about their early training. One young man said, "I knew where the line was drawn and my parents stuck to it. When I crossed it, I knew what to expect. And it made me know they cared."

I find that parents sometimes overreact to their children's conduct because they are not sure of themselves, not certain whether they should permit certain behavior or not. A harassed mother sighs, "I just don't know whether to let Kenny jump up and down on the bed like that or not." Her indecisiveness seems to make her more edgy and volatile, and keeps her house in a turmoil. Making some definite decisions will eliminate

3Romans 13:1
4James 4:7
5Ephesians 6:1, TLB

that tension. God's way is always best. If the limits are not clearly drawn at your house, it's time to establish them.

But when you do, there are a few things to keep in mind. First of all, *keep the rules to a minimum and make them reasonable.* Some parents make rules just for the sake of making rules. "It's good for them to toe the mark," they say. "They need to learn who the boss is around here." That kind of attitude doesn't teach submission; it breeds rebellion. It is usually found in a rather insecure parent who needs to boost his own ego. Will you notice please how God deals with us? The Apostle John has already taught us that loving God means keeping his commands. But he is quick to add, "And his commands are not burdensome."[6] The Lord Jesus himself said, "Come to me and I will give you rest—all of you who work so hard beneath a heavy yoke. Wear my yoke—for it fits perfectly—and let me teach you; for I am gentle and humble, and you shall find rest for your souls; for I give you only light burdens."[7]

The Christian life is not a tedious chore. It is not designed to weigh us down and discourage us with unnecessary regulations. It is a yoke that fits well, adapted to our needs. And whatever burden it may seem to be is made light by the awareness of Christ's loving gentleness toward us. We need to follow his example. The Apostle Paul must have known that fathers particularly would need this exhortation. "Fathers, do not exasperate your children...."[8] "Fathers, do not embitter your children, or they will become discouraged."[9] The Word of God gives no place to the harsh authoritarianism that some fathers mistakenly substitute for headship. They wonder why their children become bitter and rebellious when their demands have been unreasonable and unfair, and their attitude severe and unloving. Setting limits is not a miracle cure. It must be done in the proper way, even as God does it.

[6]1 John 5:3b, NIV
[7]Matthew 11:28-30, TLB
[8]Ephesians 6:4, NIV
[9]Colossians 3:21, NIV

It might be a good idea to insist on as few rules as possible, just enough to protect the child's physical and spiritual welfare, protect the rights of others, and maintain the smooth operation of the home. It is reasonable, for example, to expect a child to be home for dinner on time. His inconsiderateness here will inconvenience every other member of the family. It is reasonable to expect a teenager to drive his car lawfully and carefully. Other lives are in jeopardy, as well as his own. But since there are so many occasions when our child's will must be subservient to ours, we should avoid making an issue over nonessential things. We will need to say "no" often enough, so why not think it through and be sure it is absolutely essential before making a snap judgment. That will avoid unnecessary personality clashes that upset the serenity of the household. We parents have an uncanny way of making major issues out of trivialities and blowing potential dangers all out of proportion. We can allow some latitude in matters such as the neatness of their rooms, the clothing styles they prefer, and the places we allow them to explore with their friends. Our repressiveness or overprotectiveness, whichever it is, only creates other dangers which backfire on us in time.

Keeping rules to a minimum and making them reasonable will eliminate another problem—the impossibility of enforcing an excessive number of rules. Unenforced rules produce the same kind of tension and turmoil as no rules at all. With small children particularly, it would be far better to work on just a few rules, and when they are mastered, progress to a few more.

Second, *be sure the children understand the rules and why they exist.* This is the way God deals with us. In his Word he clearly defines our responsibilities to him. Just so, we need to let our children know specifically what the limits are. We cannot assume that they will act properly if they do not know what is expected of them. I'm afraid some kids get spanked for doing things they never knew were wrong, and that only provokes resentment.

There is a difference of opinion as to whether we should explain to children the reasons for the rules we require. Some say children need to learn unquestioning obedience to our commands, with or without reasons. That is true. But with every passing year our children become a little more intelligent and mature, and it will become increasingly important for them to know the reasons why. When the Lord demands a certain response from us in his Word, he usually tells us why. Some Christian young people have drifted away from the Lord because their parents demanded blind, unquestioning submission to certain routines and standards for which no reasons were ever given. Their inquisitive "why" was met with a belligerent, "Because I said so." That's usually a cover for intellectual laziness and it is an insult to an intelligent teenager. We may get obedience that way, but we will never build respect. And respect is the most important single factor in keeping the generation gap closed.

It may be helpful to let an older child or teenager assist in making the rules in a family council. That will make him feel more like a part of the team rather than like an obstinate outsider who is always getting picked on. And that might also be a good time to discuss the reasons for the rules and the consequences of breaking them. If he helps to establish the rules, knows why they exist, and what will happen if they are violated, he will be more inclined to cooperate.

Consistent discipline is not an easy road. All of this takes time, patience, much thought and, most of all, a close walk with God. If we look on parenthood as a bothersome chore rather than a challenging privilege, our home lives may never improve. But if we are willing to make the necessary investment of time and spiritual energies, the result will be well worth the effort. "My son, how I will rejoice if you become a man of common sense. Yes, my heart will thrill to your thoughtful, wise words... The father of a godly man has cause for joy—what pleasure a wise son is!" [10] Consider the alternative, "A rebellious son is a grief to his father and a bitter blow to his mother."[11] Is there really any question about which side you want to be on? Why not take this matter seriously and begin to clarify guidelines for your children?

[10]Proverbs 23:15, 16, 24, 25, TLB
[11]Proverbs 17:25, TLB

7
Walking
the Beaten Path

Did you ever crawl through a thick hedge? It wasn't any fun, was it? I can remember doing some undercover exploring with a couple of mischievous buddies when I was a kid, and getting so scratched up on a hedge that I hurt for days afterward. Somebody planted that hedge to keep me out, but I didn't have enough sense to heed the limits.

Kids are like that. They may be aware of the rules, but that doesn't necessarily mean they will obey them. They must be trained to live within the limits. As a teenager I worked on the coeducational staff at a summer Bible conference. The fellows and girls on staff would invariably pair off as the summer progressed. One simple rule seemed to keep us out of trouble: "Stay on the beaten path." That's what we want for our children—a disciplined walk between the hedges on the path God has for them.

Self-discipline will be essential to our children's emotional stability and personal happiness as they step out to make a life of their own, for an undisciplined person is a slave of his own passions and a victim of every circumstance. A person is only truly free when he is disciplined, much like a train is only truly free when it is on the track. But self-discipline does not come naturally. It must be learned. It is up to us as parents not only to set the course we want our children to walk, but to train them to walk it. And we have assurance from God that if we do the job properly, our children will continue to walk that course when they are grown.[1] That does not necessarily mean they will always agree with us in every detail. But it does imply that their lives will ultimately honor the Lord and so bring joy to our hearts.

But how can I help my children walk the straight and narrow path? That is the critical question every faithful parent asks. The answer should be getting quite familiar by now. We do it the same way God does. And he does it in this case by providing adequate *motivation*. God has planned things in such a way that it is pleasant for us to walk in harmony with his revealed principles, but most unpleasant when we go our own way.

In the Old Testament economy, for example, there was an elaborate system of blessing for obedience and cursing for disobedience.[2] But even in this age of unparalleled grace, with our freedom in the Spirit and our position of adult sonship, there are some interesting built-in motivations. One is the principle of sowing and reaping.[3] God allows us to experience the consequence of our own behavior, pleasant or unpleasant. And it doesn't take an intelligent person long to find out which kind of behavior yields the greatest joy and peace.

In addition to the law of sowing and reaping, God offers us some great promises of blessing for obedience. "But the man who looks intently into the perfect law that gives freedom, and continues to do this, not forgetting what he has heard, but doing it—he will be blessed in what he does."[4] God promises to prosper us when we obey his Word.

[1]Proverbs 22:6
[2]cf. Deuteronomy 28
[3]Galatians 6:7
[4]James 1:25, NIV

Then there is the further motivation of rewards at the judgment seat of Christ for good works performed by the power of
the Spirit and for the glory of the Lord.[5] God desires a mature
relationship with his children. He wants us to obey him because we love him, not to earn a reward. But in order to help us
grow toward that perfect relationship of love, he wisely recognizes the value and importance of motivation.

Now let us apply this to our role as parents. Our children
learn very early in life that certain things bring pleasure and
other things produce pain. God made them with a tendency to
continue the behavior that brings satisfaction and to discon-
tinue the behavior that brings distress. This basic principle can
provide the magic formula we need for developing in them the
behavior patterns we believe God wants them to learn. For
example, from their earliest days children find praise and appreciation most gratifying. They need it regularly. If they find
that some kinds of behavior bring them unusually large doses
of it, they will be inclined to repeat that performance. When
Johnny gets rave notices in the family circle for making his bed
neatly, for picking up his toys, brushing his teeth without
being told, or doing whatever it is we believe he should do,
he'll probably want to do it again. And we will continue to give
him that extra commendation until the behavior pattern becomes a normal part of his way of living.

In like manner, if Johnny gets laughs and applause for showing off in front of your friends, you can look forward to that
production again. He is doing what satisfies his need for acceptance and attention. Thus you are motivating misbehavior. But
if, on the other hand, he finds that his misbehavior brings him
denial of privileges or minor pain, or simply doesn't get him
what he wants, he will have a tendency to drop it.

There are a number of ways to apply this biblical principle.
For instance, money is a great motivator for teaching children

[5] 1 Corinthians 3:12-15;
2 Corinthians 5:10

to stay on the right path. I find nothing unbiblical about setting a scale of monetary rewards for fulfilling desired responsibilities. Some parents make a list of the desirable activities on a chart with seven blank squares beside each item, one for each day of the week. Every activity that is successfully accomplished each day is marked in some way, and a monetary reward granted at the end of the week for every mark. A penny a mark is sufficient for very small children, and not only provides an incentive for developing proper behavior, but also provides a base with which to begin teaching the responsible handling of money. The reward need not be money. Just stars on a chart may be sufficient for younger children. Or you may allow older children to earn some item they want very much, like a new purse or a new baseball glove.

Some parents fine their children for unacceptable behavior. My wife and I give our children an allowance and they supplement it with odd jobs. Their money is important to them and they usually spend it wisely. We decided to use it to help them learn some lessons we thought were necessary. When we began to find their belongings lying around the house and noticed their room lights on when not in use, we implemented a fine system—two cents for every personal item found cluttering up the house, and two cents for every light left burning when not in use. The money was dropped in a common bank to be used for some worthy cause. It even turned out to be fun when Dad got the first fine for leaving the light on in his study. But it was amazing to see how quickly the problems were solved when a few of their shekels were at stake.

Parents who fail to understand this basic principle of motivation find it working against them. In other words, children may use it to train their parents, and they often begin in infancy. Baby quickly learns that crying brings pleasurable results. He gets picked up, loved and cooed, changed and fed. While a baby's cry is the only way he can communicate his needs to us, we can keep him from becoming excessively fussy by refusing to cater to his every call, and by showering love and affection on him when he's not fussing.

My wife and I discovered that our little guys were pretty smart. They knew exactly how to train us. They could agitate our eardrums to such a degree we would do almost anything for relief. Then they had us where they wanted us. We finally learned to distinguish the genuine needs from mere fussiness, and refused to reward the latter. There were times when it was difficult to determine whether needs or wants prompted their crying. But we became convinced that God wanted us to try to distinguish them. He doesn't cater to every one of our selfish whims, and it is a mistake for us to cater to theirs.

Unfortunately for some parents, "Ve get too soon oldt undt too late schmart," as the Pennsylvania Dutch say. Their children begin to manipulate them in the cradle and continue through childhood and teen years. I couldn't begin to count the mothers I've known who have refused to put their children in the church nursery because they cried when they left them. So they became the victims of their children's training program. They either let the children keep them home (to their own spiritual detriment), or they brought them to the adult service (sometimes to the spiritual detriment of everyone else). When a child realizes that his mother always comes back for him and that crying won't bring her back any sooner, he'll begin to settle down and enjoy himself. It may take a few unhappy experiences to learn it, but the results will be worth the temporary unpleasantness.

Temper tantrums are another classic example of children managing their parents. Tantrums are designed by the child to accomplish something he thinks he needs. It may be to get our attention. It may be to get something else we have denied him.

It may simply be to get the satisfaction of manipulating and controlling us, since we try to control him so much of the time. And we might as well admit it—when we lose our tempers and angrily threaten him, we are not controlling him; he is controlling us. He may feel like he needs to get even with us for something we have done. Fracturing our nerves and driving us to distraction may seem to him like beautiful revenge for his damaged ego. But if he realizes that he is not accomplishing any of his goals, he will soon conclude that there is no point in beating his head on the floor in vain. So calmly walk away. Go shut yourself in another room and read a book. The act will stop when the responsive audience is gone.

Children have an uncanny ability to take their parents to the brink. They know just how far they can go, and they use that talent quite skillfully to get their own way or to do their own thing. A mother related to me that one day while she was working on something she could not easily leave, Jody and Janie, her two preschoolers, were cutting out paper dolls nearby. Janie, the younger of the two, persisted in snipping at the carpet with the scissors. "Janie, don't do that," her mother commanded. But Janie, safely out of reach, kept right on. "Janie, stop that this instant," she barked in an agitated voice. And Janie continued to ignore her. Finally her mother screamed in anger, "If you don't stop that this instant, I'm going to come over there and spank you good." Whereupon wise old Jody, a whole year more experienced than her younger sister, said, "You better not do that again. She means it this time."

You see, little Jody and Janie had trained their mother well. They didn't have to obey until she lost her temper. That gave them a little grace period to continue doing what they wanted to do without any danger of unpleasant consequences. But it gave mother a headache and put her in a terrible mood for her husband when he got home from work. Much too often an episode like that ends with mother stamping over in a rage and whaling the tar out of the child, much more harshly than she should. And the child begins to lose respect for her mother. First, because she's been able to manipulate and control her; we don't respect people we can manipulate. Second, because she isn't sure when mother means what she says and when she doesn't; her word is not really trustworthy. And third, because mother has acted in a most unloving manner.

Joe Cool Teenager is the absolute master at training his parents. Even when you know you've made the proper decision, he has a way of wearing you down with his "Fifty Famous Sayings for Getting What You Want From Your Parents." You've heard some of them: "Jimmy's parents are letting him go." "All the guys will be there." "You never let me do anything I want to do." "You did it when you were my age." "And you say you love me."

This may be followed by some door slamming and pouting. Or he may turn on the charm and become the model son. He knows what will most effectively break you down. But every time he succeeds, he loses a little more respect for you and the gap between you grows a little wider. We have already learned that we must have sound biblical reasons for our standards and that we should avoid saying "no" as much as possible. But when we know we are right before God, we need to train our children instead of letting them train us.

I have the feeling that many parents really don't expect their children to obey them the first time they speak. They expect to nag, fuss, whine, and badger to get them to do what they should. Parents who expect disobedience are seldom disappointed. Mother says to a neighbor in front of Suzie, "I just can't get Suzie to share her toys." Do you think Suzie will ever share? Not on your life. Suzie has mother well under control, helpless to do anything about her selfishness.

"I can't *make* him come to church, can I?" another parent asks pathetically. Why not? Is the standard right? If it is, then we need to insist that he observe it, and that he act properly when he's there. We don't need to be afraid of our children. God has given us authority over them and he expects us to use it, lovingly but decisively. We will answer to him if we refuse. The spoken command of a mother or father is to be carried out. God planned it that way to teach children submission to authority.

And he has given us the formula to motivate them. Once more—we are to make it enjoyable for them to obey and unenjoyable to disobey. We will explore the consequences of disobedience in the next chapter. For the present, however, just grasp the first half of the formula and learn it well. Children respond to us best when it is to their advantage. They obey us more willingly and enthusiastically when obedience is fun for them. So make it fun! Call them once in awhile when your only purpose is to give them a treat. Surprise them with a little gift for their exceptional behavior or their good grades at school.

It's not that we owe our children rewards, nor are we trying to bribe them. God's good gifts and his rewards to us are all of his grace. He doesn't owe us anything, and he certainly isn't bribing us to obey him. But the promise is still there in his Word—live in submission to him and enjoy the fullness of his blessing. And there is no end to the wonderful ways he blesses our lives when we walk in the center of his will. Let us follow his example then, and make it genuinely pleasurable for our children to obey us. There is no limit to the creative ways we can show our appreciation to them for their cooperation.

One word of warning—do not inadvertently reward unacceptable behavior. For instance, little Bobby is screaming at the top of his lungs in a restaurant, embarrassing his parents to tears. Everybody in the room is scowling at them and they wish they could drop through the floor. "Please stop crying, Bobby," mother pleads. "If you stop crying I'll give you this sucker." And presto! Bobby has discovered a brilliant new way to get a sucker. His screaming has paid off. It would have been better if Bobby's parents had planned ahead by telling him what was expected of him in the restaurant and what good things would happen as a result of his cooperation. Having forgotten to do that, however, it might have been better for them to have calmly removed Bobby from the room for a little talk, and if necessary, the kind of one-on-one contact we're going to talk about in the next chapter.

8

The Board of Education

No matter how pleasurable we make it for our children to obey us, there will be times when they break through our boundaries and go their own way. What do we do then? Once again, we do the same thing God does. We bring them back to the beaten path. "My son, do not regard lightly the discipline of the Lord, nor faint when you are reproved by him; for those whom the Lord loves He disciplines, and He scourges every son whom He receives."[1]

We've studied that word "discipline" before. It's the same word used in Ephesians 6:4 that involves both *training*, or guiding children toward a goal, and *correction*, or bringing them back when they stray. The corrective side of God's discipline is uppermost in the author's mind here in Hebrews as evidenced by the rather surprising observation that God scourges every son whom he receives. That doesn't sound very enjoyable, does it? Further on in the same context we read, "No discipline seems pleasant at the time, but painful."[2]

[1]Hebrews 12:5, 6 NASB
[2]Verse 11a, NIV

Here again is God's great motivating principle for training his children. He makes it pleasant for them to obey him and unpleasant for them to disobey, knowing that they will have a tendency to change the behavior that results in distress. That word "scourge" gives us some idea just how unpleasant God can make it. It means literally to whip or flog. God spanks every one of his children, without exception. Some will protest, "But suppose everyone doesn't need it?" Evidently every child of God does need it at some time, or God wouldn't do it. And if every child of God needs to be spanked, certainly every child of ours will need it too.

"But spanking? That's old fashioned," say the critics. Modern psychologists and pedagogues insist there are better ways of correcting children. One "expert" I read went so far as to tell his children to run if he ever tried to hit them. There are many reasons suggested for discontinuing this time-proven method of correction. Some say it teaches the child foolish and unacceptable ways of handling his frustrations. It suggests to him that he should hit when he is angry.

I know that some parents never do spank their children until they are hopping mad, but the Bible doesn't say we are to correct in anger. In fact, it says the very opposite: "Whom the Lord loves he disciplines." If we administer physical correction calmly in love as the Lord does, there is no danger of teaching our children foolish actions. On the contrary, God's Word says it will eliminate foolishness. "Foolishness is bound in the heart of a child, but the rod of correction shall drive it far from him."[3] That word rod refers to a stick, what we might call a switch. Somebody has suggested that almost everything in a modern home is controlled by switches except the children. Maybe our departure from the Bible at this point is partially responsible for the rising tide of delinquency that we face.

[3]Proverbs 22:15, KJV

When our first child was very young he received an inexpensive little toy called a Fli-Back. It consisted of a wooden paddle and a small rubber ball connected together by a long rubber band. The idea was to hit the ball successively with the paddle as the rubber band kept snapping it back. Our toddler couldn't operate it very well, and soon the rubber band broke, making the toy quite worthless—as a toy, that is. But one day, almost accidentally, we discovered an effective new use for the remnant paddle of that fractured Fli-Back. It made a perfect persuader that proved to be both safe and efficient. We had found our board of education, and it has served us well through all four children as we have applied it to their seat of learning. Strangely enough, our children's friends kept adding more Fli-Backs to our collection as birthday presents, until we had nearly enough to put one in every room of the house. I must admit, it got to be one present they opened with mixed emotions.

The "experts" cringe at such a thought. They say that using a paddle on a child will inhibit the development of his personality. "Don't repress him. He needs to express himself. That unrestrained liberty to do and say what he pleases acts as a safety valve that relieves his built-up pressures. Leave him alone and he'll turn out alright." The Bible has a little different perspective on leaving a child alone. "The rod and reproof give wisdom: but a child left to himself bringeth his mother to shame."[4] There are a good many mothers I know who are ashamed of what their children are doing. They probably followed the advice of some modern "expert" instead of the infallible Word of God and left the children to themselves, being too timid or too tired to face the challenge of enforcing limits with a rod.

Others who object to spanking say it interferes with the development of the child's conscience. Instead of rejecting unacceptable behavior, he goes ahead and disobeys, knowing he can

[4]Proverbs 29:15, KJV

pay for it with a spanking. They contend that some children go out of their way to agitate for a spanking because they know that they deserve it and it salves their conscience. If so, those children have never been spanked in a biblical manner. You may have noticed that I have carefully avoided the word punishment in this discussion. That word implies vengeance, retaliation, paying a child back for the wrong he's done, exacting a penalty which he must pay for his misdeeds. God does not punish his children. He laid all the penalty and punishment for our sins on Jesus Christ.[5] The whole debt was paid at Calvary and we have been forgiven all of our trespasses.[6] There's nothing left for us to pay. Punishment is never directed at believers. It is reserved for those who reject Christ's sacrifice for sins.[7]

But God does correct his children. We may even say he *chastens* his children, for that word implies the purging influence of his disciplinary action. His chastening hand is not intended to pay us back, but to bring us back, to restore us to the right way, to help us learn what is right and wrong, and to encourage us to choose the right. In other words, it is not punitive but productive. As the writer to the Hebrews put it, "Later on, however, it produces a harvest of righteousness and peace for those who have been trained by it."[8]

Many parents admittedly use corporal discipline in a punitive, retaliatory manner. The idea is, "You haven't told the truth, so you must pay the consequences." After they have spanked their children they consider the score to be even. But that is not God's way. He is not interested in an even score but in a holy life. His purpose is not to impose a penalty but to help us remember the right way. Administered with that purpose in view, spanking does not interfere with the development of the conscience. It sharpens it.

On one occasion after our first child was old enough to sit

[5]Isaiah 53:4-6
[6]Colossians 2:13
[7]cf. 2 Thessalonians 1:7-9
[8]Hebrews 12:11b, NIV

quietly in church and listen, my wife and I took him with us to hear a speaker we had known for years. Steve was unusually antagonistic and uncooperative that night. We tried to keep him occupied with pencils and paper, Lifesavers, pictures from our wallets, and all the other diversionary tactics we parents have learned to use in church. But he insisted on willfully and belligerently causing a disturbance. It was one of those rare occasions when I was sitting with my wife and son instead of speaking myself. And it was also one of those rare times as a rather young parent when I did the right thing. I calmly picked him up and carried him out the door, down the steps, and to the car. After a quiet and unemotional discussion about proper behavior in church, I applied the doctrine of discipline to the part of the anatomy God designed for that purpose. Then I held him as his sobs subsided, assuring him of my love and explaining that I wanted him to remember how he should conduct himself in church. After it was over we walked back to the church hand in hand, better friends than we had ever been before. It was a lesson neither one of us will ever forget, and one that keenly sharpened his ability to absorb what was said from the pulpit.

Some may ask, "But doesn't that motivate through fear? Wouldn't he behave himself in church from then on just because he dreaded another spanking?" I don't think so. Fear is used in different ways in the Bible. It can refer to a paralyzing emotion of alarm and terror, or it may refer to a healthy respect and reverence. The unbeliever has every reason to be afraid of God, with the threat of divine retribution hanging over his head. Although the believer is also exhorted to fear the Lord,[9] his is a different kind of fear. There is no anxiety or dread associated with it because it is bathed in love. The Apostle John discusses the believer's relationship with his heavenly Father: "We need have no fear of someone who loves us perfectly; his

9Psalm 34:9, KJV

perfect love for us eliminates all dread of what he might do to us."[10]

You see, the kind of fear that feels safe and secure in love is not dread at all. It's respect. Respect is wholesome and good. It's what the believer should feel toward God, and it's an essential ingredient of a good parent-child relationship. A harsh, punitive parent will command obedience by sheer terror, and raise an anxiety-ridden neurotic. But a parent who corrects in love develops a healthy respect in his child, and builds into his life the desire to obey willingly in respect to that love.

Some parents will still protest, "But I love my child too much to spank him. It seems so cruel." That is one of Satan's subtle lies. God says just the opposite. "He who spares his rod hates his son, but he who loves him disciplines him diligently."[11] They call it love when they refuse to correct their child. God calls it hate. If they really loved him, they would make sure he learned to discipline his spirit, knowing that self-discipline will affect his ability to get an education, hold a job, make a success of his marriage, get along with other people, and function adequately in other spheres of life. Corporal correction administered in love does not break a child's spirit and destroy his initiative as some have claimed. It teaches him to control his spirit, and that controlled spirit is an indispensable element of successful living. Correction furthermore assures him that you love him enough to care about his success in life. To avoid it gives him good reason to doubt your loving concern, maybe even doubt that he belongs to you. The writer to the Hebrews established that principle: "But if you are without discipline, of which all have become partakers, then you are illegitimate children and not sons."[12] The parent who refuses to spank his child is the cruel one.

Rather than being cruel, spanking is actually the kindest form of correction. It is certainly more merciful than the end-

[10]1 John 4:18a, TLB
[11]Proverbs 13:24, NASB
[12]Hebrews 12:8, NASB

less nagging, badgering, whining, and threatening that cause resentment and destroy respect. It's more merciful than weeks of denied privileges that never seem to end for the child. Of course it is unpleasant for the moment. God told us it would be.[13] It is unpleasant for the one who administers it and unpleasant for the one who receives it. So let's be honest. It isn't love that keeps us from obeying God's Word. It is the selfish desire to avoid unpleasantness. When we realize that our selfishness will only bring us greater unpleasantness over the long term, we will begin to train our children God's way.

After all is said and done, some parents are still afraid that spanking will only make their child more rebellious, maybe even turn him away from the Lord. God says, "Do not hold back discipline from the child, although you beat him with the rod, he will not die. You shall beat him with the rod, and deliver his soul from Sheol."[14] It all boils down to whether or not we believe this word from God. Those who have practiced it in the manner God prescribes have found that it works.

Well, if this is God's method, why do so many parents feel uneasy about it and guilty about it after they do it? One reason may relate to Satan's strategy. He has been calling the Word of God into question since Genesis 3:1, "Hath God said?" He wants our children undisciplined, so he plants the seed of doubt in our minds about correcting them God's way.

But that is not the only reason for guilt. Parents should feel guilty when they spank their children in anger, without love. Love is not only what we say or do, but it is an attitude our children feel. And they certainly are not feeling love when we are wildly flailing at them with popping veins and scarlet faces, when we have obviously lost control of our emotions, and our actions are retaliatory rather than remedial. Love is communicated through calmness, kindness, and control.

We may also feel guilty when we have spanked for the wrong

[13]Hebrews 12:11
[14]Proverbs 23:13, 14, NASB

reasons. Sometimes we hit because we are angered by the inconveniences which our children cause us. We have to wipe up the mess or pick up the broken glass, and it irritates us. Aren't you glad God doesn't discipline you for accidents, honest mistakes, or mere forgetfulness? We need to teach our children to be careful, but unless something like a spill is purposely malicious, it doesn't deserve a spanking.

We probably should not spank a child for his natural curiosity either, his desire to learn by touching. How much better it is to put things we don't want him to touch out of reach. I'm afraid some parents actually tempt their children by leaving expensive gadgets lying around. We encourage disobedience in other ways too, like saying to a toddler, "If you turn that pudding upside down on your head, I'll spank you." You have aroused the old nature to react, and even suggested what it should do. It would be much better to remove the bowl from the tray. There are many occasions when we can keep children from disobedience by constructive distractions or substitute activities. I believe God would be honored if we used every creative means at our disposal to keep them from disobeying.

It is self-defeating to spank a child for a nervous habit like thumb-sucking or nail-biting. That only intensifies the anxiety which caused the problem in the first place. We should not spank for unusual behavior problems caused by sickness or extreme fatigue. Nor should we spank a child for something he is not capable of doing, like sitting perfectly still for long periods of time at a very young age.

Sometimes a child's rebellious behavior grows out of fear or insecurity. If he feels threatened or unloved, it would be far better for us to listen patiently and try to understand his feelings than to spank him. The spanking will only make him feel more threatened and less loved. Spanking should be reserved for direct defiance of our authority, willful disobedience to our command, or a willful attitude of stubborn rebelliousness, none of which are caused by extenuating circumstances. It takes a Spirit-filled Christian walking in fellowship with the Lord to have the wisdom necessary to know when spanking is in order and when it is not.

We may also feel guilt for spanking when we have been excessively harsh. If we get exasperated with our children we may lash out with greater intensity than their deed deserves. The guilt we feel may be God's way of warning us of the damage we are doing both to them and to ourselves. Make the correction fit the crime if you want to enjoy a clear conscience before God. Sometimes we prescribe foolish punishment in a fit of rage. Don't be afraid to say, "I'm sorry," then lighten the sentence.

We should also add that there are other effective means of discipline besides spanking. God is not stereotyped and there is no reason for us to be. The biblical emphasis on the rod does not necessarily eliminate other methods of correction. Different personalities and degrees of responsiveness may dictate different approaches. If Johnny loses the use of his tricycle for a few days because he insists on riding it in the street, he will quickly learn the boundaries. If he finds himself isolated in his room every time he teases his sister, he will probably decide that teasing is not very profitable behavior and drop it.

Teenagers will profit more from other forms of discipline. There comes a time in life when spanking may only harden and embitter a young person, and other methods of correction will become more effective. In other words, it is possible to wait too long to apply the rod of corrective discipline. "Discipline your son in his early years while there is hope. If you don't you will ruin his life."[15]

Verbal reproof alone may be sufficient on some occasions, but it must be done in love. Forget the angry lecture with all the

---

[15]Proverbs 19:18, TLB

usual threats. They only breed rebellion. The kids realize the threats are empty, and they know the whole lecture by heart anyway. Just do it God's way. It is not always the easiest way, but let him help you move in with the appropriate correction, calmly, kindly, lovingly—but immediately and firmly. "Discipline your son and he will give you happiness and peace of mind."[16]

[16]Proverbs 29:17, TLB

9
Whose Problem Are You Solving?

Do you have the answer, or are you part of the problem? That penetrating question has been known to stop people short in their tracks and make them face their own personal responsibility in some tangled relationship. Maybe it's time we parents asked it honestly about ourselves. We're grappling with the problem of training our children, but there may be some flaws in our approach that need to be ironed out first. The converse may also be true. There are times when we think we are training our children when, in reality, we are working on our own unresolved conflicts.

In order to help us get our problems and our solutions properly sorted out, I would like to suggest four brief but pointed principles to govern the course of child-training in the Christian home.

1. *Be positive.* Read through the New Testament epistles sometime for the sole purpose of learning what God expects of you as a believer in this age of unsurpassed grace. You will find a few "don'ts," but the overwhelming majority of God's

commands are positive. When we begin *doing* what God wants us to *do*, the "don'ts" usually take care of themselves.

Unfortunately, some parents have adopted the Colossian heresy as their guiding principle for training their children: "Do not handle! Do not taste! Do not touch!"[1] It's "Don't do this" and "Don't do that" from morning 'til night, until the poor child must wonder if it's even safe to breathe. And he becomes enmeshed in a cobweb of fears and anxieties with a negative outlook on life and a set of inhibitions that keep him tied up in knots most of the time. Learn to put things positively whenever possible: "Billy, use your fork, please," rather than "Don't you dare eat with your fingers!" "Linda, straighten up your room now," rather than "Don't you set foot outside that room, young lady, until every one of those toys is in its place!"

By being positive, we are not suggesting the endless nagging that wears children down and grates on their nerves. "Comb your hair. Straighten your tie. Button your coat. Stand up straight. Hold your shoulders back. Tie your shoelaces. Hurry up, you'll be late." That's a disguised form of criticism that springs more from our own needs than the child's. We are simply saying that instruction is more acceptable when it springs from a positive spirit.

This will virtually eliminate the negative criticism many parents continually offer. God's standard is high—his own holiness. But he knows our weaknesses and he doesn't continually pick at us and fuss at us for our failures. In a passage about God's forgiveness, the Psalmist says, "For He Himself knows our frame; He is mindful that we are but dust."[2] The Apostle John said, "My little children, I am telling you this so that you will stay away from sin. But if you sin, there is someone to plead for you before the Father. His name is Jesus Christ, the one who is all that is good and who pleases God completely."[3] "But if you sin...." That's a rather understanding attitude, isn't

[1]Colossians 2:21, NIV
[2]Psalm 103:14, NASB
[3]1 John 2:1, TLB

it? We need to have it when our children fail to live up to our expectations.

Criticism is one of the most disheartening elements of life. We all know what it means to do the best we can, only to have somebody find fault with it. It makes us feel inferior, guilty, and worthless; it destroys our confidence and saps our ambition. Yet many parents feed their children a constant diet of negative criticism. "Is that the best you can do?" "Well, I see you finally cleaned up your room. Now go do it over again." "Is a B the best you can do in math?" Or worse yet, when one of those inevitable accidents occur, we exclaim in exasperation and anger, "Can't you do anything right?"

George was a young man with a fractured ego. He told me it had been his regular chore to keep the basement clean when he was a boy. With a coal-burning furnace, coal dust, ashes, and dirt would cover the rough concrete floor. Often when he finished, his father would take the broom from him and sweep up another pile of dirt, berating him for the poor job he had done. Some years later he discovered that it was possible to get dirt off a floor like that only after four or five sweepings. But it was too late to salvage his sagging confidence.

How much more effective it is to encourage children with warm and sincere commendation, to express confidence in their abilities and optimism about their progress. "That's a good job, son. You're doing better every time." "Say, you brought that C up to a B this time. Good for you." Children need encouragement. In fact, it may well be the most important factor in their growth toward emotional maturity and stability. Our proneness to criticize and our unwillingness to commend are reflections of some unresolved problem in our own lives. It may be a rigid demanding perfectionism, a lack of personal self-confidence, a desire to make ourselves look better, or maybe even a fear that our children's achievements will surpass our childhood accomplishments. All of these are insidious expressions of pride. Our critical spirit is the feeble attempt of the flesh to compensate for our weakness. When we let the Lord deal with that pride, we shall be free to accept our child's weaknesses, and will then be able to help him overcome them by encouragement rather than compound them by criticism.

2. *Be calm.* Several times in this book I have mentioned keeping calm and avoiding anger. Some may be wondering why that is so important. After all, doesn't the Bible speak about the anger and wrath of God? If God gets angry, why can't we? Maybe it is necessary to draw another distinction. Just as we have differentiated between punishment and discipline, and between fear and respect, so we need to distinguish fleshly anger from righteous anger.

God's anger cannot possibly be a sinful emotion because God has no sinful nature. Rather than a flaring of emotion, God's anger is a settled opposition to sin. There is no trace of anxiety, resentment, or hostility in it, but only indignation over sin and its effects. It is not selfish, but essential to his own infinitely holy nature. God's anger is righteous and good.

A Christian can have that kind of God-like anger, as when his righteous indignation over sin or injustice moves him to constructive and helpful action. But it will always be unselfishly motivated by the wrongs committed against others rather than himself, and it will be free from anxiety, resentment, and hostility. That is probably what the Apostle Paul meant when he said, "In your anger do not sin."[4]

Too many parents are kidding themselves when they try to categorize their anger as righteous indignation. They are just flat steamed up—mad, hurt, and hostile. They're venting their spleen because they've been irritated, inconvenienced, embarrassed, exasperated, or challenged, and the old sin nature is hanging out all over the place. When they lose their temper

[4]Ephesians 4:26a, NIV

they're dealing with their own problem, not the children's, and they're not handling the problem very successfully.

God has a few things to say about this fleshly emotion. "Stop your anger! Turn off your wrath."[5] "Let all ... wrath, and anger ... be put away from you...."[6] To differentiate the two, wrath is the boiling outburst of temper, while anger is the smoldering coal. Neither one has any place in the life of a Christian parent. "For man's anger does not bring about the righteous life that God desires."[7] God has dealt with me about this, so much so that I finally asked my children to tell me when I sound angry with them. They usually forget, but the offer still stands. I need all the help I can get to overcome the sin in my life, including help from my children.

The Apostle Paul commanded us not to provoke our children to anger.[8] What is it that stirs up a child's anger? Let the Word of God answer the question. "A gentle answer turns away wrath, but a harsh word stirs up anger."[9] Children react just as adults do. When somebody talks to them in angry tones, it makes them resentful and rebellious. It's like rubbing sandpaper on their emotions. Then when they get angry, it makes their parents more angry, and the vicious cycle ends in a verbal brawl from which nobody benefits. If the child gets hit in that rage, it increases his fear and deepens his hostility. And whether he gets hit or not, he usually becomes more sullen and unresponsive and loses respect for the parent whose emotions he can arouse like a plaything.

When the temptation to be angry threatens us, it's time to get alone with God and resolve it. If some form of correction is necessary, send the child to his room and tell him you will be there in a few minutes. Then go to your room, get on your knees before God, and ask him to dissolve that rising tide of emotion and replace it with his calm. That will prepare you to discipline your child effectively, for his good rather than your own.

5Psalm 37:8a, TLB
6Ephesians 4:31, KJV
7James 1:20, NIV
8Ephesians 6:4
9Proverbs 15:1, NASB

"He who is slow to anger is better than the mighty, and he who rules his spirit, than he who captures a city."[10]

3. *Be consistent.* A faulty pattern of discipline is all too typical in many homes. It goes something like this. Little Billy is paying no attention to his mother's instructions because he has learned to tune her out. That's easy to do. When I was a boy, I lived one block from the major railroad line between Philadelphia and New York. Visitors in our home found those trains offensive, but I seldom heard them. We learn to tune out unpleasant sounds and that's exactly what Billy is doing. His mother's first command is nothing more than an irritating sound. It doesn't mean anything at all, so he ignores it.

Then mother begins to nag. "I wish you would learn to obey me, Billy. Why can't you ever do what you're told the first time I speak? I don't know what I'm going to do with you." Billy is now feeling a secret surge of satisfaction because this big strong woman can't control him. But all the while, mother is repeating her command, her pitch is getting higher, her decibel level is increasing, and her anger is rising. Sometimes Billy can read her perfectly and hops to it just before her fuse ignites, especially if she gives him that "One ... Twoooooo ..." routine. On other occasions his timing is slightly off and she explodes in a rage of verbal and physical abuse. Naturally, she feels guilty because of her excessively harsh punishment, so the next day she tries to compensate by letting Billy get away with almost anything. And Billy is systematically learning the art of juvenile delinquency, losing respect not only for his mother, but for all authority. "Because sentence against an evil work is not executed speedily, therefore the heart of the sons of men is fully set in them to do evil."[11]

The solution to this tragic situation is consistency. Correction must regularly begin at the first sign of disobedience. When we speak once in normal tones, we should expect obedi-

---

[10]Proverbs 16:32, NASB
[11]Ecclesiastes 8:11, KJV

ence. If we do not get it, then we move in immediately to correct the disobedience. There are no empty threats, no increasing degrees of anger, no rising crescendo of shouting, just the calm, kind, loving, but firm insistence that we be obeyed when we speak. The rod will then become associated not with retaliation but with love, the loving concern that our children learn the joy and blessing of a disciplined spirit.

Consistency requires more self-discipline on our part than anything else. Raising our voices is easier than getting up, walking over, and administering firm but loving correction at the first sign of disobedience. But God will help us if we let him. The fruit of the Spirit is self-control.[12] Self-control involves the ability to do the right thing at the right time. And the right time for correction is at the moment of disobedience. We are to apply the rod "betimes,"[13] meaning early or when the need exists. When we allow the Spirit of God to deal with our problem of laziness, we shall be able to discipline our children his way.

Consistency also involves changelessness in maintaining our standards. This is the way God deals with us. "I am the Lord," he says. "I change not."[14] Rules must be flexible, and exceptions will be made in extenuating circumstances. But generally speaking, if we are going to insist on a certain code of behavior one day, then we ought to insist on it the next day as well. To require it one time and ignore it another bewilders children.

Conversely, to let them get away with something most of the time, then suddenly to punish them for it in a fit of anger, defeats our aim of teaching them self-discipline. When we decide to train our children God's way, we should first give them some explanation of why we expect this standard of conduct and how we intend to help them remember it. Then when we do need to correct them, we again remind them of why we expected their obedience, how we are now going to help them

[12]Galatians 5:22, 23
[13]Proverbs 13:24, KJV
[14]Malachi 3:6, KJV

remember, and what they can do in the future to avoid this unpleasantness. This kind of instruction accompanying correction will begin to transform the reason for the child's behavior from the mere pleasant or unpleasant effects of it, to a healthy respect for us and for others.

Consistency, furthermore, means agreement between father and mother on standards of behavior and methods of correction. Some of the most rebellious kids have grown up in homes where mother and dad have been sabotaging each other's authority. One may have been overly strict and the other overly permissive, and each one was trying to equalize the other's excesses. The inevitable result was a lack of respect for either. The kids soon learned how to get what they wanted by playing one parent against the other. That kind of situation will be averted when mother and dad discuss discipline together ahead of time and agree on the rules and how to enforce them. Even when harmony does exist, the kids may occasionally succeed in getting different verdicts from mom and dad separately. That's the time to back up, have a private high-level conference, and agree.

Consistency will likewise involve keeping our word. If we make a promise and attach no conditions to it, we should not break it as a disciplinary measure. To do so is to teach our children to break their word. Some promises cannot be kept due to circumstances beyond our control, like rain on the day of the picnic or a sudden emergency that demands our attention. Those occasions can be used to explain the difference between breaking promises and being hindered by circumstances from doing what we want to do. Life is filled with disappointments, and our children must learn how to cope with them very early in life. Our gentle spirit at such times will help. But nothing can take the place of a child's inner confidence that his parent's word can be trusted.

Consistency means fairness too. Our children each have different personalities and different degrees of maturity, so exactly the same rules and methods of discipline may not always apply to every child. But we need to be as uniform as we possibly can. I can still hear the plaintive cry of several young people with whom I have counseled who were sure their parents didn't care for them. The reason? The standards set for them were different from those set for their brothers or sisters, and the discipline they received was far more severe. God is just in dealing with his children,[15] and we should be with ours.

4. *Be loving.* We devoted an entire chapter to love for our children, but a brief word needs to be repeated in this context of discipline. Even when the rod strikes, our children should feel love as much as pain. Before we correct them, we will want to explain why our love requires us to do this. After we correct them, we will hold them close and continue to assure them of our love. God will use our love to encourage love in them, until they grow to the point of obeying not just to avoid unpleasantness, but because they genuinely love the Lord and us. And this is the goal of maturity toward which we are building.

One of the saddest mistakes a parent can make is to threaten his child with the withdrawal of his love. "Mommy won't love you if you do that." A cutting comment like that grows out of mother's own insecurity, and the emotional scars which it leaves will be a long time healing. God does not threaten to withdraw his love from his children. He keeps on loving them even when they sin. To the nation Israel he said, "I have loved you, O my people, with an everlasting love."[16] When we love our children with his kind of love, it will never cease.[17] Then our discipline will eventuate in their profit rather than express our problems, to the blessing of all.

---

[15]Psalm 89:14
[16]Jeremiah 31:3, TLB
[17]1 Corinthians 13:7, 8

10
Bugs and Butterflies

Somewhere along the pathway of parenthood I got knocked off my parental pedestal. I don't remember the exact age of my oldest son when it first happened, but one day I suddenly realized that I was no longer the know-all, do-anything hero figure I once had been in his eyes. In fact, he knew more than I did about some things and he seemed to enjoy gibing me about my shortcomings. I suspect that my fall occurred somewhat earlier with my succeeding children due to his influence around the house.

What happened? Did I change? No, I don't think so—at least not for the worse. If anything, I probably matured a little. Well, then, did he change? Not necessarily. He just began to develop the ability to see things as they really were. You see, two of the ferocious features of the species called "adolescent" are a keen sense of perception and brutal honesty, often to a parent's chagrin.

I have noticed something else about my teenagers. They are subject to extreme variations of energy and temperament for no apparent reason.

They have sudden bursts of limitless vigor, as when playing touch football with their friends. But at other times they seem to be too tired to get off the couch and go to bed. Sometimes they astound us with their maturity and insight, while on other occasions we are dumbfounded at their childishness and foolishness. The experts tell us that these fluctuations are caused by the momentous changes taking place in their bodies and are perfectly normal. That might help us keep calm, if only we could remember it when they are acting in an emotional and illogical manner, or giving us static about something we want them to do.

But the fact remains, there are moments when we are enjoying the company of a delightful adult and other times when we are tolerating the antics of a selfish child, and it's the same bundle of bones and chromosomes. The whole bizarre phenomenon reminds me of one of nature's most magnificent transformations—the metamorphosis of a crawling caterpillar into a gorgeous butterfly. And some days our kids seem to resemble the bug more than the butterfly. Actually, they are neither children nor adults. They oscillate between the two, groping to establish their identity. We can help them immeasurably by viewing them not as struggling children but as emerging young adults.

The Model Parent endures something much like the teen years with us. Who of us would not admit to periodic lapses into childishness along our road to spiritual maturity? The most mature Christians will honestly acknowledge that they still have moments of stubborn selfishness. Yet God patiently and lovingly encourages us to keep on growing toward the likeness of his Son.[1] And he views us in the light of what we someday shall become by his power and grace.[2] That assurance is a great motivating influence in our spiritual progress. If we want to bring our teens to maturity in the Lord, we will let God

---

[1] 2 Peter 3:18
[2] e.g. Philippians 3:20, 21;
1 John 3:2

give us his attitude of encouragement and expectancy in place of our attitude of consternation and condemnation. And the teen years will not be a burden to dread but a blessing to anticipate. We shall look forward to them with the bright hope that our teens will emerge as beautifully mature adults.

Even with our attitudes properly adjusted, however, we need to be reminded of some principles that will help us guide our teens successfully through these difficult years. I say remind because we already know what to do. If we have been functioning to this point as God's Word outlines, very little will change. The example we have set will be as important as ever. The love we show, while becoming less physical in its expression, will continually be given in large doses. The warm relationship we have established and continue to nurture will help keep that infamous generation gap from splitting wide open. The discipline we have maintained, while offering wider freedom and greater responsibility than previously, will continue to be a necessary part of their training. We will keep implanting the Word of God into their minds to provide direction through life and delight in living. In other words, we began to lay the foundation for these years from the day our children were born, and we keep building on that foundation now that they are teens.

Some folks have asked me what they should do when they assume the guardianship of teenagers, such as foster children or relatives, and have not had the benefit of providing all that early training themselves. The only possible answer I know is to begin where they are and follow the principles of the Word with them. If you find yourself in that situation, this letter from just such a woman may reassure you.

When we were in our early twenties the Lord sent us sixteen-year-old Sharon, juvenile hall runaway. We had no special insight nor experience. We were forced to use God's love and Word. A few months later, the Lord sent sixteen-year-old Robin to us. We used the same tools. Five years later came sixteen-year-old Gwen and twelve-year-old Ron. There were times when we were sure things weren't going to work, but as we went to the Word we were encouraged to continue.

We couldn't start at point A as we did with our three natural children, so we began with them right where they were. All four have received Christ. Two are now married. One is preparing for Christian service. We've seen their personalities transformed by the power of Christ and today they are beautiful sojourners, waiting and watching for their Lord. It works!

With that helpful word, we are ready to be reminded of some matters that need to be emphasized when dealing with teens. For one thing, *we must keep the lines of communication open.* One of the most common complaints of teens against their parents is, "My folks don't understand me." Communication is more than talking. It is understanding the other person's ideas and feelings, and accepting his right to believe and feel the way he does. Acceptance does not necessarily mean agreeing with all his opinions nor approving of all his emotional expressions. But it does mean accepting him even if his opinions differ from ours, and respecting his right to feel that way.

This is one of the hardest things for parents to do. When our kids have different ideas from ours, we conclude that if they are right, we must be wrong. And for them to imply that we are wrong is to attack our intelligence and self-esteem. So we fight back and angrily defend our opinions. And if we don't have the facts to support our point of view, we try ploys like, "Look, I'm older than you, I know what I'm talking about, and that's the

way it is. The sooner you admit it, the better off you'll be." And zap! All communication is cut off.

Our tactic has implied that our teen is immature and stupid, that his ideas are vastly inferior to ours, and that the only real basis for communication is his conformity to our viewpoint. It will be a long time before he subjects himself to that kind of insolence again. How much better it would be to say calmly and kindly something like, "Yes, I can understand why you feel that way. But let me share a few other thoughts for you to consider as you work this thing through in your mind."

Sometimes our teen's announcement of what the kids at school are saying or doing, or what he himself has done or would like to do, is met with shock, anger, or a tedious lecture. Plain old common sense tells him how to avoid that kind of unpleasantness—simply by keeping his mouth shut. On other occasions we find ourselves rattling off our preconceived and prejudicial opinions without ever hearing him out or trying to understand exactly what he has said. He doesn't have to be very brilliant to figure out that we are not really interested in what he thinks, only in what we think. Soon he'll stop sharing what he thinks.

God has some good advice in this area of communication for parents of teenagers. From the Old Testament comes this profound pronouncement: "He who gives an answer before he hears, it is folly and shame to him."[3] Parents, we must learn to control our mouth muscles while we sharpen up our auditory nerves.

The Apostle James added his inspired advice. "My dear brothers, take note of this: Everyone should be quick to listen, slow to speak, and slow to become angry."[4] Nothing destroys our teenagers' respect for us faster (and builds more tension or breeds more rebellion) than our quick-triggered, angry reactions. We can expect a certain amount of argument and dis-

---

[3]Proverbs 18:13, NASB
[4]James 1:19, NIV

agreement from them. They are trying to find themselves, trying to discover who they are, and what they can or cannot do. But when we lose our temper, they know that they are stronger than we are. They discover, if they never realized it before, that they have the power to control our emotions, and the fight is on! We must learn to listen with both ears open, patiently, calmly, attentively, acceptingly, and understandingly.

Understanding does not mean soft sentimentality, however. We will still state our opinions and the reasons for them, but we will do it lovingly. We will still forbid disrespectful back talk, but not with an impulsive slap and an indignant "Don't you talk to me that way." Instead we will explain that we understand how they feel, but we must insist that they learn to express their feelings courteously. Their unwillingness to comply will result in denial of privileges or other forms of correction, administered firmly but lovingly. We will still expect compliance with the rules and family routines we believe are proper, but it will be with the growing desire to increase their freedom and personal responsibility.

That need for greater independence brings us to the second general principle. *We must treat our teens with respect.* We owe them that from their earliest days, but it takes on a new complexion as the teen years blossom. Another common complaint teenagers make against their parents is, "My folks treat me like a child." That accusation is often founded in a parent's basic lack of respect for his budding young adult, and this too can sow the seeds of rebellion.

Lack of respect may come to the surface in a variety of ways. For example, parents may refuse to allow their teen the freedom to make decisions for himself. From minor issues such as which clothes to buy, to major matters like what college to attend, parents sometimes force their desires on their young person. God gave him a mind, and we should respect his right to use it to find God's will for his life, rather than forcing him into our mold. Of course we will offer scriptural advice when he is tempted to move away from the plan God has clearly revealed in his Word, but we will seek God's wisdom to know when to speak and when to be silent.

Another indication that respect may be lacking is parental ridicule of adolescent awkwardness or physical peculiarities. It isn't his fault that his voice cracks or that his face is covered with pimples. Those telltale signs of his incomplete development haunt him enough without our magnifying them. A word of encouragement or some constructive advice would be far more fitting.

Sometimes we have a tendency to laugh at the problems which he considers important, like the ups and downs of his love life or the disagreement he's had with his friends. Maybe they do seem a little trivial to us, but a sincere respect for him would help us look at the problem through his eyes and sympathize with him. We often forget how important those same problems were to us when we were his age. All we seem to remember about our youth are the things that help us prove our point. "When I was your age I never ..." And almost every parent has finished that sentence in a variety of ways. Don't do it! It really doesn't matter what we did or didn't do when we were his age. Times have changed, and we need to respect our young people for who they are in this day and time.

There are a number of positive steps we can take to show them our respect. We will keep the confidences they share with us. Divulging them to our friends often has a way of coming back to haunt us. We will respect their privacy, knocking before entering their rooms and keeping our noses out of their personal belongings. We may want to ask their advice about something, especially when they know more than we do about it. I asked my teenagers' opinion of this chapter before I tried it out on anybody else. We may want to take them into our confidence to show them how much we value their friendship. And we will trust them to the limit of what our Lord will permit us.

That matter of trust raises a difficult point. There will be times when our prayerful judgment will demand that we pull in the reins and say "no" to something they want to do. It may be an overnight with a family we do not know, or a trip with some guys of questionable character, or an amusement of doubtful moral implications. But we have no peace about allowing it. The first maneuver of our insistent offspring will probably be, "Don't you trust me?" How do we deal with that?

The answer to that question may be something like, "Yes, we trust you to the limits of your ability to resist temptation. But if we have any reason to suspect that a situation may apply more pressure than you can withstand at your present level of spiritual strength, then we have an obligation to God to keep you from it." You see, trust is a mutual thing. We must have a growing trust in them and in their desire to please the Lord when away from our watchful eye. But they in turn must trust our desire to do what is best for them in questionable circumstances. One without the other is unfair.

And this leads us to our final principle. *We must provide biblical reasons for our standards.* There are so many doubtful things in our dirty world. How do we decide what we will allow and what we will not allow in matters such as movies, music, dancing, fashions, hair, and friends?

It is vital to recognize that we live in a changing world. While God doesn't change and his eternal principles remain constant, the application of those principles may vary from age to age and from culture to culture. We need to be willing to reexamine and reevaluate our value systems. Too often we demand that our young people submit to our inflexible rules just because we have traditionally followed them. There may be no solid biblical support for some of those standards, but we rigidly impose them upon our teens anyway. And it has been shown to incite a spirit of rebellion in some of them.

Some parents tell their youth they cannot do certain things because "Christians don't do that," or "Our church doesn't believe in that." But the kids know better. They know that some Christians are doing those things, maybe even some in their own church, and they see the fallacy of our reasoning. But when young people have biblical grounds for the standards set for them and they see a consistent example in our lives, they will be more likely to maintain those values when they are free from our authority, and not indiscriminately taste everything the world has to offer.

Here then are four biblical suggestions for deciding doubtful things. The first is the principle of *liberty*, that is, freedom from anything that might bring us under its power. The Apostle Paul wrote, "All things are lawful for me, but I will not be mastered by anything."[5] Any enslaving habit, anything we find that we must have or must do, which we cannot easily give up when we want to, is not acceptable behavior for a Christian. We cannot be controlled by the Holy Spirit and by the things of the world at the same time. And we parents must set the pace. A parent who tells his teen not to drink or smoke while he himself indulges is in for trouble.

The second principle is that of *love*. True Christ-like love lives for the benefit of its object rather than itself. Since believers are exhorted to love one another,[6] it follows that we ought to live for each other's advantage. "Let's please the other fellow, not ourselves, and do what is for his good and thus build him up in the Lord."[7]

The Apostle Paul personally felt at liberty to eat meat that had been dedicated to idols. After all, the idol meant nothing to him. But he denied himself that privilege lest a weaker Chris-

[5]1 Corinthians 6:12b, NASB
[6]John 13:34
[7]Romans 15:2, TLB

tian for whom it would be idol worship follow his example and fall into sin. We are not faced with the problem of meat offered to idols, but there are other things we might personally feel free to do that could lead a weaker Christian into sin. "Be careful, however, that the exercise of your freedom does not become a stumbling block to the weak."[8]

The third principle is that of *edification*. "All things are lawful, but not all things are profitable. All things are lawful, but not all things edify."[9] Not everything we feel we can do will make a worthwhile and strengthening contribution to our physical or spiritual lives. It may be harmful to our bodies which are the temples of the Holy Spirit. But even if it doesn't actually harm us, it may monopolize time, waste money, and dissipate energies that should be more profitably invested elsewhere. God knows that we all need diversionary recreational and relaxing activities to be at our best for him. And every believer has to apply this principle to his own life individually by the direction of God's Spirit. But parents have a responsibility to give their teens some godly guidance in employing it, both by instruction and by dedicated example.

The fourth principle is that of *exaltation*. God says we belong to him, and everything we do should show off his goodness, glory, and grace. "So whether you eat or drink or whatever you do, do it all for the glory of God."[10] Our manner of life should say to those around us, "See how wonderful my God is—how holy, how loving, how gracious, and how kind!"

This is a high level of living to attain. But how can we do less than grow toward it for a God who has forgiven our sins, freely given us eternal life, and come to dwell within us. "Haven't you yet learned that your body is the home of the Holy Spirit God gave you, and that he lives within you? Your own body does not belong to you. For God has bought you with a great

---

[8] 1 Corinthians 8:9, NIV
[9] 1 Corinthians 10:23, NASB
[10] 1 Corinthians 10:31, NIV

price. So use every part of your body to give glory back to God, because he owns it."[11]

When Young People Go Astray

In spite of our best efforts, there may be instances when a young person insists on defying our authority and going his own way. The promise of Proverbs 22:6 is inviolable, but there are some critical years between the time we train the child "in the way he should go" and the time "when he is old." Satan is going to dangle the enticements of the world and the flesh before him during those years and make sin just as attractive as he possibly can.

Jesus told a famous story about a wayward son and it provides some practical help for parents who face that crisis in their homes.[12] It is important to note in Christ's parable of the prodigal son that *the father did not forcibly restrain his son from leaving home.* While younger children can be dissuaded from running away, there comes a time in the life of an older adolescent when physical force will not prevail. If your child has determined to give his life to debauchery and degradation, he is going to find the opportunity to do it one way or another. So let him go. Let him make it on his own. As long as he lives under your roof you are financing his rebellion, and that isn't helping him at all. You should sit down with him, calmly point out the pitfalls of his choice, and lovingly warn him that God will deal with him as a son. But if he persists in his course of sinful self-will, there is no point in trying to stop him.

Notice secondly in the parable that *the father let his son bear full responsibility for his actions.* He didn't take the blame personally and he didn't run to bail him out of his scrape. Not one of us will be an absolutely perfect parent, but God doesn't want us to torture ourselves with guilt over the way we have

<hr>

[11]1 Corinthians 6:19, 20, TLB
[12]Luke 15:11-32

raised our child. He wants us to acknowledge our failures and enjoy his gracious forgiveness.[13] In spite of our parental shortcomings, our child must answer to God for his own actions. He cannot blame his parents for his decisions. If he chooses the path of sin, he does it of his own volition and he must live with the consequences of his choice. "Yes, each of us will give an account of himself to God."[14]

Notice thirdly that *when his son repented, the father welcomed him home with true forgiveness.* There was no attempt to shame him nor belittle him, just a genuine expression of love and concern for his well-being. When our wayward one gives evidence of repentance, we too need to forgive and welcome him home. And with true forgiveness, we will not try to make him suffer for the embarrassment and heartache he caused us with questions like "How could you do this to your mother and me after all we've done for you?" We cannot condone his sin, but we must show him that he is more important to us than our feelings or our reputation. Such forgiving love is more than the world can offer and may be used of God to bring some unbelieving onlooker to himself. If that should happen, those agonizing days, or years, will culminate in two-fold joy—the joy of our child being restored to us and the joy of a new child being born into God's family.

[13]1 John 1:9
[14]Romans 14:12, TLB

11
Dad's Many Hats

It was thirty minutes later than usual when Harry Hasselmore turned into his driveway after work. The contracts his boss requested at the last minute had given him a late start for home and he had gotten caught in that miserable freeway traffic jam. The heat was unbearable and his head was splitting. A good dinner and a quiet evening of relaxation—that's what he needed.

"What are those bikes and wagons doing in the driveway?" he fumed to himself. "I've told those kids a thousand times to put them where they belong." Harry spied the kids in the neighbor's yard and screamed, "Get over here and put these things away. You kids are getting more irresponsible every day." It didn't seem to matter that their friends were standing there listening to his embarrassing tirade. As they crossed the yard, Harry spied the rip in Ralph's jeans. "Look what you've done!" he yelled. "You kids must think I'm made of money."

Leftovers for dinner didn't help his disposition much, and he grumbled through the whole meal.

It never occurred to him that Helen had used considerable creativity and much time to make those leftovers appetizing and save him some money. And then the kids—their manners were always atrocious but it was particularly annoying tonight. Harry rose to the occasion in this characteristic manner: "Don't eat so fast. Don't talk with your mouth full. Will you please stop smacking your lips. Do you have to lay all over the table? Stop this confounded bickering at mealtime! Can't you kids give me any peace?"

He had just sunk into his easy chair with the newspaper when Joanie said, "Daddy, will you fix my doll house?" "Not tonight," he snapped. "And besides, if you were more careful with your things they wouldn't get broken." He didn't notice the hurt on her face as she walked slowly to her room.

Just about then Ralph came bouncing in. "Hey, Dad, wanna play catch with my new ball?" "When are you kids going to learn that I have more important things to do than play, play, play?" Harry growled. It had been a long time since Ralph had asked his dad to do anything with him. It would probably be quite awhile before he asked him again.

"Harry, I must talk to you about the children." Helen was finished with the dishes now and desperately needed his advice on what to do about the children's latest malicious neighborhood prank. "Look, Helen, get off my back, will you? Whatever it is, I'm sure you can handle it. Now leave me alone tonight." While the day may have been a little worse than usual, Harry's attitude was not much different. He was becoming increasingly irritable and impatient, and while not realizing it, he was systematically destroying his family. His wife was getting discouraged and depressed, and his children were becoming more and more of a problem.

The Bible reveals that Harry holds the key to correcting this tragic situation. You see, not only has God set us a perfect example of fatherhood to follow, he has also said some pointed things in his Word about a father's responsibility in the home. But until Harry opens his mind to these truths and expresses a willingness to obey them, there is little hope of improvement. A father's role is not an easy one. It is momentous and many-sided. We must understand the many hats dad wears and learn how to wear them.

First of all, he is to be a *leader*. Nowhere is that more succinctly stated than in the divinely established qualifications for an elder in the church. "He must manage his own family well and see that his children obey him with proper respect. (If anyone does not know how to manage his own family, how can he take care of God's church?)"[1] That word *manage* means literally "to stand before" and therefore "to preside over." God has placed fathers in the family to take the lead. God's authority in the home centers in dad.

In many cases, dad thinks he is the head of the house, and mom may even let him believe it. But in reality she manages nearly everything. Most of the time he doesn't even know what's going on. Sadder still, he may not even care. He likes the arrangement that way because it takes the responsibility off his shoulders. She decides what the children can or cannot do. She checks on their schoolwork, talks to their teachers, and signs their report cards. She helps them work out their problems, teaches them what they need to know, and takes them where they need to be. Dad is little more than a disinterested bystander who yells at them once in awhile to make his presence felt. And the result is calamitous.

Studies have shown that there is a direct correlation between a weak father figure and a child's problems in areas such as character, conduct, and achievement. Those who work with teens in trouble invariably discover the lack of an adequate father image in the home. There are indications that the major-

---

[1] Timothy 3:4, 5, NIV

ity of men who fail in executive capacities come from homes with unsatisfactory father figures. When dad abdicates his position of authority in the home, mom usually assumes the role she was never intended to have. The unhappy combination of a disinterested father and an overbearing mother can drive children to run away from home, enter early and unwise marriages, or suffer emotional difficulties and personality deficiencies.

Dad must take the lead. But what is involved in properly managing a family? For one thing it means taking the lead in providing physical necessities, such as food, clothing, shelter, and medical care. Paul used masculine pronouns in referring to these kinds of things when he said, "If anyone does not provide for his relatives, and especially for his immediate family, he has denied the faith and is worse than an unbeliever."[2] Mother may work, but the primary responsibility for meeting the family's needs falls on dad. Indolent fathers who refuse to accept this responsibility need to heed this severe indictment.

That is only the beginning, however. He also takes the lead in instructing the children—interpreting the great events of our day in the light of the Scripture and teaching them how to live in conformity to God's Word. The Psalmist refers to this fatherly function. "For he gave his laws to Israel, and commanded our fathers to teach them to their children...."[3] The Apostle Paul likewise mentioned it. "For you know that we dealt with each of you as a father deals with his own children, encouraging, comforting and urging you to live lives worthy of God, who calls you into his kingdom and glory."[4]

Father should take the lead in conducting times of Bible study and family worship, in encouraging family involvement in the ministry of a local church, and in establishing the family's testimony in the community. Far too often dad just doesn't care about spiritual things and mother takes the lead, leaving the kids with the twisted notion that the church is a woman's

---

[2]1 Timothy 5:8, NIV
[3]Psalm 78:5, TLB
[4]1 Thessalonians 2:11, 12, NIV

world and spreading the gospel is women's work. When dad becomes the source of spiritual strength in the home, children and youth begin to get serious about the Christian life.

In the final analysis, properly managing the home means overseeing everything. That doesn't mean dad is a dictator, running everything with an iron hand, making every decision and doing everything himself. As a godly manager, he prayerfully considers the feelings of others and his decisions are for their good rather than his own. He recognizes his wife's abilities and encourages her to develop them and use them to their fullest extent. But she makes sure that he is aware of what is going on, and that he approves. And to be assured that he is in charge, that he has final responsibility for the smooth operation of the household, and that he will faithfully discharge that responsibility, brings a great sense of security both to her and to the children.

Not only is father to be a leader, however. He is to be secondly a *lover*. He must love his wife with an unselfish, forgiving love, a love that transcends all loves but that for Christ himself. Somebody has suggested that the very best thing a father can do for his children is to express a Christ-like love toward their mother. The idea is biblical. Paul exhorted husbands to love their wives as Christ loved the church.[5] When God established the institution of marriage he said, "Therefore shall a man leave his father and his mother, and shall cleave unto his wife: and they shall be one flesh."[6] Children would come, but a husband and wife should always enjoy a very special closeness to each other.

Simply stated, Dad, that means that after the Lord himself, your wife comes first in your life—before you, before your boss, before your friends, before your Christian service, even before your children. And those very children will be the beneficiaries of your faithful adherence to this principle. Your love for their

[5]Ephesians 5:25
[6]Genesis 2:24, KJV

mother, openly expressed, will give them a sense of satisfaction and security that nothing else in this world can provide. They may groan and cover their eyes when you take her in your arms and kiss her, muttering something like "Oh, brother, here we go again." But deep down inside there will be a warm glow of contentment. Mom and dad love each other.

Some husbands and wives live only for their children and they never really get to know each other. One day, all too soon, the kids are grown and gone and mom and dad are left staring at each other like total strangers with nothing to say, toying with an uncontrollable urge to meddle in their children's marriages. Meanwhile, the kids are feeling the psychological pinch of over-dependence on their doting parents. Their adjustment problems in marriage are enormous, and the pulls and pressures from home make it even more difficult to work them out. Psychologists have verified that parents who enjoy a loving relationship with each other have the best prospects for untroubled and resourceful children who establish successful marriages of their own.

So, Dad, take your wife out for dinner periodically. Bring her something that says "I love you." Spend time talking about the things that are burdening her. Be sensitive to her needs and live to meet those needs. Help her with her chores. If she's had a particularly hard day, cheerfully take over and encourage her to go out for awhile. Don't knock her or argue with her in the children's presence. Be demonstrably affectionate toward her in front of the children. How else are they going to learn how to love?

The most frequent answer I received, when I asked college students in what way they felt their parents might have failed them, was lack of love between their parents. One girl wrote, "No affection was ever shown in our family, my father toward my mother or my parents toward us. I know I can't blame them totally, but I am not a very warm, receptive person." Some had never seen any open expression of love between their parents and were suffering from emotional malnutrition as a result.

One of the best things you can do for your wife is to park the kids someplace and get away by yourselves for a few days—just the two of you. Constant responsibility has a tendency to drain us, physically and emotionally. God can give us grace to handle the pressures of life, but he may want us to use our common sense and get away from them periodically. Jesus recognized that need. "The apostles gathered around Jesus and reported to him all they had done and taught. Then, because so many people were coming and going that they did not even have a chance to eat, he said to them, 'Come with me by yourselves to a quiet place and get some rest.' "[7] It is often easier to evaluate a situation and see ways of improving it when you stand off from it for awhile. Being apart will help you renew your spirits, remove the little tensions that tend to build up in the confinement of a house, and give you time to understand each other and an opportunity to clarify your goals and purposes for the children. It will draw you closer to each other and closer to them. And there is nothing at all wrong with looking forward to the day when the children will be on their own and you will be able to enjoy each other, alone.

The third major role a father must play is that of *disciplinarian*. King Solomon revealed that it is the father who corrects or reproves his son.[8] Paul reminded those fathers who aspired to be elders to see that their children obeyed them with proper respect.[9] Furthermore, he addressed fathers in that great passage which outlines the broad spectrum of child-training: "And fathers, do not provoke your children to anger; but bring them up in the discipline and instruction of the Lord."[10]

Why did Paul direct this exhortation to dads? As we noted earlier, the first half of the exhortation may be addressed to

[7]Mark 6:30, 31, NIV
[8]Proverbs 3:12
[9]1 Timothy 3:4
[10]Ephesians 6:4, NASB

them because they are more prone to the harsh and hostile aggressiveness that angers and exasperates children. A fatherly rule by force and fear breeds the same personality and conduct problems as no father image at all. It may produce an angry rebel who lashes out against society, or a guilt-ridden misfit who feels unworthy and rejected. We need to heed Paul's advice to the Colossians: "Fathers, do not exasperate your children, that they may not lose heart."[11] Good discipline begins with self-discipline, not with a loud mouth or a lot of muscle.

But the positive side of the command is directed to fathers as well: "Bring them up in the discipline and instruction of the Lord." We are driven to the inescapable conclusion that dad is ultimately responsible for the entire process of child-training. He is accountable even for what mother says and does to the children. He answers to God for everything that happens in the home. As God's authority figure, he must know what is going on and be in control.

This has some obvious practical ramifications. For one thing, dad should handle the discipline when he is home. In most cases, mother has the job of child-training all day. When dad walks through the door, she should know that her shift is over. He will protect her from many of the pressures and problems she has grappled with alone through the day. Furthermore, since she has represented his authority while he has been out of the house, he must support her and uphold her before the children. And in view of his many hours away, he must spend time talking to her about what has happened, offering Spirit-directed advice and help. That is a tall order, but the end is not yet.

The fourth role God would have every father fill is that of *companion*. That doesn't mean pal. Some fathers have made fools of themselves palling around with their kids and trying to do everything they do, often to the embarrassment of the

---

[11]Colossians 3:21, NASB

younger generation. By companion I mean comrade, confidant, and friend. Who can deny that fathers generally are alienated from their children in our society. Isn't it interesting that in the last revelation from God in the Old Testament era, the prophet Malachi announced concerning the forefunner of Messiah, "And he shall turn the heart of the fathers to the children, and the heart of the children to their fathers...."[12]

While this passage still awaits its final prophetic fulfillment, it illustrates what God's grace can accomplish even today in restoring a cherished relationship between fathers and their children. God wants them to be of one heart, one mind, and one soul. That will require time spent together, with open communication and intimate communion. Boys and girls both need time alone with dad. It might be in the form of lunch or dinner out together, a picnic, a hike, a fishing trip, a tennis match, or any other fun experience that will provide opportunities to talk and get to know each other. Mother can help by not demanding so many material things that dad must work day and night to pay for them, and consequently never see his children. She can also help by not begrudging dad's time alone with the children. But with the time available and mother in full sympathy, it will simply be a matter of disciplining himself to do it. An ideal occasion for communication and companionship with younger children is at bedtime. Dad needs to lay down his newspaper or turn off the TV and put the kids to bed periodically. He cannot afford to miss the opportunity for informal romping, meaningful conversation, and spiritual input available in those moments before they are tucked in for the night.

A boy particularly needs to know his dad. Dad represents the man he will become—the husband he will be to his wife, the father he will be to his children, the provider he will be for his family, the leader he will be in his church, and the witness he will be in the world. He needs an example to follow, a model to

[12]Malachi 4:6, KJV

identify with, a dad he can be proud of. Sons tend to repeat the pattern set by their fathers in marriage. That's a fearful thought, isn't it? Give your son a good standard to emulate. Sometimes when the father image is weak or missing, a boy tends to cling to his mother too long. When he is grown he looks for a wife who will continue to mother him, and the next generation marriage is a disaster. Dad, spend time with your boy.

We all know that death and divorce have robbed many a boy of his dad. What do we do in those cases? All through the Bible God encourages a unique concern for the "fatherless." That emphasis may reaffirm how vitally important this father image is. Studies have shown that substitute fathers in organizational relationships can go a long way toward meeting this emotional need of boys. Christian men need to open their hearts to fatherless boys.

Daughters too need to know their dads. A girl learns from her dad what men are like. He represents the husband she will one day give herself to, the father of her children, the authority figure she will submit to. It has been observed that a girl often subconsciously seeks a husband like her father. So, become the kind of husband you want your daughter to marry. Then cultivate a warm and cordial relationship with her. It will help her adjust successfully to the husband God gives her. If you deprive her of your companionship, the resentment she feels will be transferred to other men, even to her husband. And the weight of your failure will rest heavily upon you for years to come.

Isn't all this too much for one mere mortal man to be and do? Yes, it is. The demands on his time will be relentless. The drain on his emotional resources will be unending. But the last role God requires of a Christian father will provide him with the strength to become everything else God wants him to be. He must be a *man of God.*

A father's authority to manage his home comes from God. But he cannot exercise that authority properly unless he subjects himself to the authority of God. Paul explained to the Corinthians that just as man is the head of the woman, so Christ is the head of man.[13] Some men are not fit to manage their homes because they are not in submission to the Word and will of Jesus Christ. They can never be all that God wants them to be so long as the flow of his power is restricted by sin.

Jesus taught us the secret of living in fellowship with him just as a branch lives in the vine. Then he said, "If you remain in me and my words remain in you, ask whatever you wish, and it will be given you."[14] The formula for our success as fathers is filling our minds with God's Word, then spending time in his presence seeking the willingness and power to obey it. As we grow in his likeness we shall fulfil our roles with wisdom. "I have told you this," Jesus added, "so that my joy may be in you and that your joy may be complete."[15]

[13]1 Corinthians 11:3
[14]John 15:7, NIV
[15]John 15:11, NIV

12
The Majesty
of Motherhood

Majesty? Mother hardly feels like her royal highness as she stands beside her messy sink, harried and haggard from the battles of the day. Before she can take the weight off her tired feet, she still faces that stack of dirty dishes, a load of dirty diapers, three dirty kids who must be bathed and put to bed, and a dirty house that must be cleaned for the ladies' circle in the morning. Waves of resentment, self-pity, then guilt sweep over her. She feels more like a captive than a queen ... and so far removed from that model mother of Bible times whose husband and children stand up and praise her as the greatest among women.[1]

Motherhood is undoubtedly one of the most complex and exacting callings in life. A poll among women revealed overwhelming agreement that raising children properly requires as much intelligence and drive as holding a top position in business or government. And that task falls mainly on mother's shoulders for the first six years of the child's life. Even after that, her contacts with the children will of necessity be more frequent and prolonged than dad's. While dad is the leader in the house, mother sets the tone. The hours her children spend in her presence will have a lasting influence on their lives. They will become largely what she makes them. She faces the noble challenge of molding their young lives for eternity. Motherhood is one of life's highest honors, and one of its heaviest responsibilities.

Where does a woman find help for such an awesome assignment? The Psalmist said it well: "My help comes from the Lord, who made heaven and earth."[2] God has special grace for mothers. You see, even though God is a father, he has a mother's heart. He spoke to the nation Israel and said, "I will comfort you there as a little one is comforted by its mother."[3] God comforts his children just like a mother.

It is the third person of the Trinity, the Holy Spirit of God, who basically performs this motherly function. Jesus called him the Comforter,[4] and sent him to us so that we would not be orphans.[5] And isn't it interesting that our birth into the family of God is described as being "born of the Spirit?"[6] The Spirit of God who bore us, who shared his divine life with us, who sustains us, comforts us, and teaches us, stands ready and willing to aid every Christian mother in fulfilling her sacred duty.

By observing the ministry of the Holy Spirit, a mother will be able to detect her first responsibility. The Spirit proceeds from both the Father and the Son, and ministers not on his own behalf but for them. Jesus said, "... for he will not be presenting his own ideas, but will be passing on to you what he has heard. He will tell you about the future. He shall praise me and bring me great honor by showing you my glory. All the Father's glory is mine; this is what I mean when I say that he will show you my glory."[7]

You see, the Spirit is submissive to the Father and the Son, and represents them in his ministry to us. Just so, *a mother is to*

[2]Psalm 121:2, NASB
[3]Isaiah 66:13, TLB
[4]John 14:26
[5]John 14:18, NIV, TLB, NASB
[6]John 3:5, 6, 8, KJV
[7]John 16:13-15, TLB

be *submissive to her husband and represent his authority to the children.* Failure here has become one of the major causes of family disruption and breakdown. When a woman resists the will of her husband, it weakens his self-respect, discourages him from taking the leadership role in the family, and destroys the order of authority God established for the home.

Furthermore, a dominant wife and mother confuses the children. The Lord Jesus established an important principle, which he applied fundamentally to money but which can be applied with equal force to the family. "No one can serve two masters. Either he will hate the one and love the other, or he will be devoted to the one and despise the other."[8] If mothers and fathers have equal authority, the child does not know which one to obey. He will use one against the other to get his own way, and will soon lose respect for one or both parents. Studies have shown that children with conduct problems often have domineering, high-strung mothers. But if a child knows beyond all doubt that dad is the head of the house, that mom speaks for dad, and that dad's authority backs up what she says, he will be more apt to obey and will have more love and respect for both his parents.

The biblical injunction to wives to submit to their husbands has far-reaching implications. The repeated emphasis on it in the Word gives some indication of the importance God lays upon it.[9] Successful parenthood depends upon successful husband-wife relationships. And successful husband-wife relationships rest heavily upon a wife's respect for her husband and her cheerful submission to his will. Her authority over the children is derived from him. If she undermines or contradicts his authority before the children, she is destroying her own authority. If she outwardly or inwardly rebels against his authority, her children will sense it and develop the same kind of rebelliousness toward her.

[8]Matthew 6:24, NIV
[9]Ephesians 5:22, 24;
Colossians 3:18;
Titus 2:5;
1 Peter 3:1, 5

Mother, cultivate a deep appreciation and loving admiration for your husband. Next to your personal relationship with the Lord Jesus, he comes first in your life. If he isn't the husband he should be, don't nag him, push him, or pick at him. That will only drive him farther from you. If things between you aren't what they should be, don't wrap yourself up in your children to compensate for the insecurity and lack of love you feel from him. That will only damage the children's personalities and further destroy your relationship with him. Look for his good qualities and rehearse them in your mind. You will find your respect for him growing. And when he senses that growing respect, he will work to make it grow even more. Before long you will be able to add a few more items to that list of qualities to appreciate. Your marriage will improve, and your freedom to be a good mother will enlarge right along with it. Some wives have complained to me that they cannot think of any good qualities in their husbands. But something attracted them to those men originally. Think back to those early days of courtship if need be, and magnify the commendable traits you remember.

The second major responsibility of a mother is likewise learned from the Holy Spirit, this time from the name Christ gave him—the Comforter.[10] The word literally means "one who is called in beside." It suggests the ability to help, encourage, and console. Just so, *a mother is to be near her children, providing assistance, encouragement, and comfort.*

The Apostle Paul referred to this motherly function. Describing his ministry to the Thessalonians he said, "… we were gentle among you, like a mother caring for her children. We loved you so much that we were delighted to share with you not only the gospel of God but our lives as well, because you had become so dear to us."[11] "Caring for" means literally "to keep warm." Figuratively, it involves cherishing and comforting. A

---

[10]John 14:16, 26; 15:26; 16:7
[11]1 Thessalonians 2:7, 8, NIV

mother instinctively longs to press her child to herself, protecting him from danger, soothing his hurts and easing his pain.

As natural as that longing may be, it is sometimes dulled by the pressures of life, by a selfish spirit, by the lack of personal security, by seething hostility, anxiety, or unresolved conflicts with others. Mother may allow herself to become irritable and sharp with the children, creating an unpleasant atmosphere of tension and discord. You see, she is the one who actually establishes the mood of the home. Father may be its head, but as many others have suggested, she is its heart. Her emotional state will often become the condition of the entire household, and even the youngest child will absorb the effects of it. A child's mind is like a video tape recorder, carefully transcribing every word, right down to the tone of voice and facial expression. And all of it contributes to the person he will become. Some psychologists say his emotional pattern is set by the time he is two years old. That should be a sobering realization to mothers, and a challenge to examine carefully their attitudes and temperament. A change for the better will have a profitable effect whenever it comes.

Mrs. Pickit is obsessed with having a perfectly clean house. Her conversation consists of "Pick this up, put that away, straighten those things, scrub that better." Fussing has become an automatic, involuntary way of life for her. She may ultimately drive her child to the opposite extreme of sloppiness, or may produce in him the same neurotic perfectionism she has.

Mrs. Skelter is a disorganized person who is always running late. She keeps the household in a state of turmoil screaming at everyone to hurry up. A child who lives with that kind of pressure becomes tense and troubled. He does poorly in his schoolwork and finds it difficult to get along with other children.

Mrs. Wartner is overly anxious. She worries, frets, whines,

and stews about every little problem, actual or potential. And every one of those fears is registering on the consciousness of the little tyke beside her, building a spirit of apprehension and anxiety that will hold him in bondage for a lifetime, but for a miracle of God's grace.

Mrs. Grumpman is unhappy and dissatisfied. She complains about her plight in life. She grumbles about the way people treat her. She gripes about the inconveniences she suffers. And little ears send impulses to little minds around her making discontentment the habitual pattern of their lives as well.

A child needs someone near him who loves him more than the house, whose heart is bubbling with the joy of Jesus Christ, who displays an inner calmness even during the trying circumstances of daily living, someone who is patient and kind, who encourages and cheers. Mother, the Spirit of God can make you that kind of person. Flee to his presence often during the day and claim his wisdom and strength.

Then spend time with your children. Read to them. Teach them the Word of God. Take casual walks with them, pointing out interesting things along the way. Play games with them. Create challenging things for them to do. Take an interest in their projects. Be available when they need you. And like the Spirit of God, be sympathetic and compassionate. Your children will someday stand up and praise you for it.

Working Mothers

The thought of mother being near her children raises the question of whether or not she should be gainfully employed outside the home. It would be difficult to prove from Scripture that it is wrong for a mother to work. That model mother in Proverbs 31 certainly did. "She finds wool and flax and busily spins it.... She goes out to inspect a field, and buys it; with her own hands she plants a vineyard. She is energetic, a hard worker, and watches for bargains. She works far into the night.... She makes belted linen garments to sell to the merchants."[12] Women did contribute to the family income in Bible times.

It has been shown from Scripture, however, that dad has the primary responsibility of providing for the physical needs of his family. Before a wife goes to work, I would suggest that she and her husband sit down together and answer some pertinent questions. First of all, *why do they want her to work?* If it is because she is bored with her role as a mother, working may not be the answer. She needs to rethink her attitudes and face the challenge of motherhood. To do that job as God wants it done, particularly with younger children, can tax all of her intelligence, utilize all of her skills, and consume as much time as she is willing to give it. If her motive is to buy herself more clothes or even to purchase some luxury for the entire family, maybe both she and her husband need to readjust their priorities according to God's Word. If on the other hand it is to help with the necessities of life, contribute to the children's education, or provide some other needful thing, the Scripture would not forbid it.

But there is a second question: *Will she be able to fulfil her task as a homemaker happily?* The Apostle Paul exhorted women to "guide the house,"[13] one word in the original text meaning "to manage the household, to keep house." He also told them that they were to be "keepers at home,"[14] a similar word meaning literally "working at home." In other words, God intended for the wife and mother to be the homemaker. She has the basic responsibility of tending to the affairs of the household. Homemaking can easily become a frustrating part-time avocation for the working wife, to the detriment of the entire family. A husband who loves her and is sensitive to her

[12]Proverbs 31:13, 16-18, 24, TLB
[13]1 Timothy 5:14, KJV
[14]Titus 2:5, KJV

needs will want to help around the house, but willing assistance is far different from being assigned his share of the household duties as sometimes happens when a woman works. That is a reversal of the roles which God established for husbands and wives. When it is essential for mother to work, dad should mobilize the whole family to lend a hand. The kids can learn some vital lessons in teamwork and responsibility through it.

Question number three: *What will the actual advantage be?* Don't forget to count everything: federal income taxes, state income taxes, social security taxes, God's percentage, baby-sitting if necessary, additional clothing, transportation, lunch and coffee break money, costlier meals (if she buys more prepared foods or TV dinners with no leftovers). Some couples have actually found that they lost money when mother went to work.

The fourth question is the most important of all. *How will it affect the children?* For some children, coming home to an empty house encourages dependability and maturity. For others it breeds insecurity and presents temptations to get into trouble. Baby-sitters may help, but no baby-sitter will give a child the love and attention that mother can provide. If the children are all in school, a part-time job that allows her to be home when the children are there may be the answer.

This is an issue about which husband and wife must agree. If a wife takes a job against her husband's wishes, the door is open to more serious problems. Seek God's direction together with a deep desire to do his will, and he will surely guide.[15]

Single Mothers

Divorce is one of the great tragedies of our times, but it is very much with us and ignoring it will not make it go away. In

---

[15]Proverbs 3:5, 6

many cases children are involved, producing a large corps of single parents. Add to their ranks the widows, widowers, and unwed mothers and their number is enormous. The vast majority of these single parents are women, and so we direct a brief word to their plight here. The comments we make should be equally applicable to single fathers, however.

Not long ago I had the opportunity of addressing several questions to a group of Christian singles about their parental problems. Most of them were divorced. When I asked what advice they would give to someone who had just become a single parent, one woman wrote, "If possible, don't become one." That's the best advice I know. God has the solution to every marital problem. If there is any hope at all of a reconciliation, seek it diligently whether or not the divorce is final. With godly counsel and a willingness to work at the marriage there is hope for success.

For the widowed, that advice is meaningless. And for many of the divorced, it's too late. What then are the problems of single parenthood? One recurring theme was *loneliness.* "Eight or nine P.M. comes, your child is in bed, and you are alone. There's no one to share burdens and joys with. You have the responsibility of rearing a child. But that child cannot meet you at your level of communication. Often that loneliness turns to self-pity."

What is the answer to this gnawing empty aloneness? Another single writes, "Join a caring group of single parents who are interested in the welfare of the children in addition to their own social needs, especially a Christian group." Family outings with such groups will expose your children to adults of the opposite sex and help fill the void in their life. More important for you personally, it will provide opportunities for fellowship with adults. Contact with adults who have similar problems to yours will meet some of the needs in your life and will help you relate better to your children when you are with them. But the best remedy for loneliness is to cultivate a growing relationship with the Lord. He has promised never to leave you nor forsake you.[16]

A second common problem was *having the time, energy, and patience to meet the needs of the children.* A woman writes, "Often it seems there is never enough time in the day just to be Mama. For example, having just finished a hard and hectic day at the office, now it's time to pick up my daughter from nursery school. She's been playing and learning happily all day and is unaware of my frustrations (as she should be). She's so excited to see her Mama. She wants Mama all to herself. But Mama is tired. And it's time to make supper, wash dishes, do some cleaning. Then it's time to get her ready for bed. Where has the time gone? A single parent has to do the work of two. Yet her child needs the love and reassurance that only she can give. Is there time?"

The same single mother answers her own question. Mark it well! "Your child needs you, his parent, *now*—not when you have the time, but now. Therefore, you must make the time. Share your activities with the child, let him be your helper. It's not easy, for sure, but so very necessary."

The third most frequent problem cited by divorced parents relates to their ex-mates and the *bitterness* that remains between them. There always seems to be a temptation to put the blame for your troubles on your former mate and make that one look bad in the child's eyes. A single dad offers some good advice: "Don't criticize the 'ex.' Encourage the children to love and respect the other parent. And do everything you can to make it clear that the children are not responsible for the breakup." One divorcee told me that every night when she prayed with her son at bedtime, she assured him that God loved him, she loved him, and daddy loved him. In spite of the

---

[16]Hebrews 13:5

calamity of divorce, that little fellow enjoyed a healthy relationship with his father.

There is only one way to reduce the lingering pain of divorce and to heal some of the wounds that endure. "Get rid of all bitterness, rage and anger, brawling and slander, along with every form of malice. Be kind and compassionate to one another, forgiving each other, just as in Christ God forgave you."[17]

Single parents and their children are needy people. It would be to the credit of every complete Christian family to reach out with Christ-like love to help meet those needs. Some children of divorce have never seen a happy marital relationship. We can invite them to our homes and show them that marriage can be a wonderful experience. God may use us to help build successful homes in years to come.

[17]Ephesians 4:31, 32, NIV

13
Learning to Fly

It's a big day in a bird's life when he first begins
to fly. His mother senses his readiness as he
squirms, stretches his neck, and twitches his
wings. She may lure him from the nest by holding
a tempting tidbit a short distance away, or she
may encourage him to take to the air with a gentle
nudge. In either case, he flaps for his life on that
maiden flight and, because of her prodding, is
soon soaring off alone to explore the wide world
around him.

Sad to say, birds have more sense than some
human parents. Our feathered friends seem to
know that the aim of caring for their young is to fit
and furnish them to leave the nest, while many
parents seem to be unaware that some day their
children must leave home and make it on their
own. They invest precious little time or effort in
preparing them for an independent life. The kids
suddenly find themselves as young men and women, facing the prospect of leaving home, ill-
equipped to hold a job, handle their money, or
succeed at their marriages. These are skills that

must be learned, and the best way to learn them is from their parents in the home.

God handles this matter in his family framework. He provides us, his children, with the resources and the abilities we need to function successfully in the Christian life.[1] His indwelling Holy Spirit endows us with the abilities we must have for our respective responsibilities.[2] Then he trains us in his Word so that we shall be able to exercise those abilities profitably unto all good works.[3] We need to take our cue from the Master Homebuilder and help our children develop the ability to operate capably in their various roles in life.

One obvious way we strengthen their wings for flight is by letting them make an increasing number of decisions for themselves. Those decisions will be as significant as possible at each level of growth. At first they may be as simple as choosing the clothes they put on in the morning. But as they grow older they will be doing such things as choosing their own friends, earning and managing their own money, buying their own clothes, and deciding which extracurricular activities they wish to engage in. If we have taught them properly and they have learned the biblical principles by which decisions are to be made, we can trust them to choose wisely and grow to maturity through practice.

We all learn best by doing, but doing inevitably involves making some mistakes. Our children will make their share, and we should not become overly concerned about it. The Lord allows us to exercise our wills and learn by our errors, doesn't he? He is always available to give direction and to help us do what is right, but he doesn't smother our independence nor coerce us to conform. He lays the responsibility for our actions upon us. We should follow a similar course.

Our children's lives will be filled with choices and decisions for which they will be responsible and for which they will pay

[1] 2 Peter 1:3
[2] 1 Corinthians 12:11
[3] 2 Timothy 3:16, 17

the consequences. We must let them start with small choices and grow, rather than jump into the stream of life at age twenty-one with no decision-making experience, and slowly but surely sink. We will lengthen the cord of freedom with each passing year, and finally let go. That full release is often the hardest part. The unwillingness of parents to cut their children loose has wrecked more young marriages than most of us would care to admit.

One of our children came up with a perceptive insight as he got ready to spend his first night away from home at a friend's house. At just seven years of age, he was suffering some apprehension over this new adventure. We could almost see the wheels turning in his head when suddenly it all came out: "I understand," he said, "when I was a baby you put me in the nursery. When I got a little bigger I went to the older nursery, then to the Beginners' Department. Then one day I spent a day away from home, now a night, someday a whole week, then a month. And when I'm a man I'll be able to stay away from my mom and dad." He saw it almost clearer than we did. Parents, start lengthening the cord and preparing your children for freedom.

Now, in addition to this growing liberty to make decisions, there are several specific areas of understanding and responsibility, crucial to successful living, which should be taught in the home. The parents who train their children in these four areas are laying the groundwork for future happiness. Each area deserves far more consideration than we can give it here, but we shall seek to establish at least a few basic principles for each.

Learning the Dignity of Work

If we want our children to grow into mature, dependable adults, we will need to give them personal responsibilities.

Happy people are people who have something to offer. They know they belong; they fit in; they are worthwhile members of the unit rather than dead weight. The Lord sets the pace again by assuring his children of their importance in the family. Every member of the body of Christ has a function to perform. Peter said, "God has given each of you some special abilities; be sure to use them to help each other...."[4] We would do well to follow his example.

Those who sit idly by thinking the world owes them something are usually miserable, maladjusted people who hate themselves and cannot get along with others. And most of them never learned the dignity of work when they were growing up. One college student frankly admitted to me, "I wish my parents had given me more responsibilities and work to do when I was younger. Now I'm fighting to correct my bad habits of laziness and lack of self-discipline." So teach your children the blessings and benefits of honest labor. Use the Scriptures. God has a great deal to say about the subject.[5]

Then put the Scripture into action by letting your children contribute in tangible ways around the house. Give them jobs to do, chores for which they are responsible—not necessarily for money, but just as their share in the smooth operation of the household. Even small children can keep their rooms tidy and empty the wastebaskets. As they get older they can make their beds, set the table, clear the table, help with the dishes, sweep the patio or garage, push the vacuum, carry out the trash cans, help with the yard work, wash windows, wash the car, and a host of other things that need to be done. Not only will it teach them how to work, but it will take some of the pressure off mom and dad and free them to give a little more attention to being the kind of parents they ought to be. You might also want to encourage them to seek other jobs outside the home, like delivering newspapers, mowing lawns, running errands, sacking

[4]1 Peter 4:10, TLB
[5]e.g. Genesis 2:15; 3:19;
Proverbs 6:6-11; 10:4, 5;
Ephesians 4:28;
1 Thessalonians 4:11, 12;
2 Thessalonians 3:10-12;
1 Timothy 5:8.

groceries, or baby-sitting. Some of the greatest men and women in our nation's history learned the discipline of work when they were young.

There are several guidelines we need to follow, however, when teaching our children to work.

1. *Show them how to do the job you are asking them to do.* Sometimes we take for granted that our children know things we have never taught them, and then we scold them for not doing it the way we want it done. A few minutes of instruction will eliminate that tension. And while you are instructing them, instill in them a deep appreciation for a job done properly. Solomon said it: "Whatever you do, do well...."[6] Everybody's time has been wasted if the job has to be done over.

2. *Teach them to work hard and happily.* That seems to be what Paul had in mind when he said, "Whatever you do, work at it with all your heart, as working for the Lord, not for men."[7] When they go to work for someone else their time will not be their own. It will belong to their employer. If they use every minute of it profitably and take genuine pleasure in doing the job well, they will be sought after and paid well. A number of businessmen have complained to me in despair, "I just cannot find people who want to work." Young people who have learned to enjoy working are at a distinct advantage in the job market. But more important still, the Lord is honored when we give a job our best with a cheerful spirit. All necessary work is really work for him and should be performed with that in mind, whether the boss is looking or not.

3. *Teach them to think while they work.* If they keep their wits about them they will be less apt to make costly mistakes or cause serious injuries. With their minds in gear, they may see more efficient ways of doing the job, or see other things that need to be done so that they can fill their working hours honestly and productively. This resourcefulness, carefully culti-

[6]Ecclesiastes 9:10, TLB
[7]Colossians 3:23, NIV

vated at home, will often bring advancement in the working world.

4. *Teach them to finish their jobs.* Some people's lives are littered with unfinished tasks, incompleted projects, and shattered dreams. They hop from job to job, unable to find happiness in any vocation. They may even lack the willpower to stick at making their marriages work and run home to mama at the first sign of trouble. They never learned to find satisfaction in staying with a task to the end. Their parents let them quit whenever the going got tough and they are still quitting. If your child begins a project, even something of his own choosing like making a model airplane or painting a picture, encourage him to finish it.

Applying these simple principles should go a long way toward preparing your children to take care of their needs in life. It may be wise to add one word of warning, however. Don't expect perfection. Even though we want the job done right, we must remember that children are still children. We can expect them to perform according to their capabilities, but to demand more will be frustrating and discouraging to them. It is distressing for a child never to be able to please. Compliment the acceptable aspect of the job even if it isn't perfect. Let him know you are grateful for his effort.

Appreciating the Value of Money

The logical sequel to learning the dignity of work is learning how to manage the money we earn. There is nothing sinful about making money. In fact, we cannot live without it. And since its proper use will be vital to our children for meeting their physical needs, maintaining their personal self-esteem, and making their marriages succeed, we owe them some instruction in this area.

In order to learn how to handle it, they first must have some. Their money will come from two primary sources, the first being an allowance. If parents can possibly afford it, they ought to give their children a small amount of money each week as a base for this learning experience. An allowance is not pay for doing chores. Chores are their contribution to the household team just as mom's and dad's are. An allowance is their share of the family income, and the amount they receive will vary with their age. Second, they may supplement their allowance with odd jobs, either at home or outside the home. If a child wants to earn extra money by doing things around the house beyond the call of duty, let him. If you are going to pay someone else to do it anyway, why not keep the money in the family?

Now that they have some money, teach them to use it to the glory of the Lord. Three general principles should help.

1. *Teach them to give a generous portion to the Lord's work.* They cannot afford to miss the exciting benefits God heaps on faithful stewards. Try this promise on for size: "Give, and it will be given to you. A good measure, pressed down, shaken together and running over, will be poured into your lap."[8] It's not that we give to get. That kind of selfishness squelches the joy of it all. We give to glorify God. But he appreciates our obedience so much that he recycles our gifts back to us in increasingly abundant ways. "Remember this: Whoever sows sparingly will also reap sparingly, and whoever sows generously will also reap generously."[9] If we really believed that word from God, the ten percent we hear so much about might become just the small beginning of a great new adventure with him. Even if your toddler only gets a dime a week, teach him to give a generous portion of it back to the Lord.

2. *Teach your children to save as much as they need for future plans.* Those famous "easy payments" have destroyed far too many marriages. How much more sensible it is to earn

---

[8]Luke 6:38a, NIV
[9]2 Corinthians 9:6, NIV

interest on our money by saving for the depreciable items we need. And the time for our children to learn that is when they are young. Insist that they put a portion of their money in a savings account. It will bring them immeasurable personal satisfaction to save for that new bicycle, or to have that money for camp when the anticipated week arrives. And what will make their college education more meaningful than paying for some of it with money they themselves have saved?

3. *Teach them to spend the rest with wisdom and gratitude.* The gratitude part is not too difficult. They can usually thank the Lord for the joy of having money to spend. But wisdom is a little more difficult. That involves sorting out their wants from their needs. It's their money, and they can spend it on personal pleasures if they desire. But if they spend it all on frivolous non-necessities the first day, they may have to do without some of the things they need for the rest of the week. That's alright. Let them live with the consequences of their actions until the next dole is due. Experience is a great teacher. And it's far better to learn this lesson with nickels and dimes than with boats and campers and similar items that cost thousands of dollars.

Wisdom also involves buying at the best price. Teach them how to shop to get the most for their money. Take them to the stores with you and show them how to compare. Wisdom also means avoiding waste. I remember having dinner at the home of a very wealthy Christian businessman. Before we sat down to eat the steaks he had just barbecued, he took a pair of tongs and dropped the pieces of burning charcoal into a bucket of water one by one so he could use them the next time he cooked out. I began to realize why the Lord could trust him with so much money. I had known that he gave a good portion of it back to his church, and now it was obvious that he didn't waste very much of it either.

Seeing that your children have a moderate amount of money

and teaching them how to use it will circumvent two damaging pitfalls. The first is the indignity of having to beg you for every penny they need, and that is damaging to their self-esteem. The second, probably far worse, is the indulgence of getting everything they want. Somebody has quipped, "Money isn't everything in life, but it sure helps you keep in touch with your kids." Parents who try to maintain contact with their children by giving them material things usually suffer the recurring heartache of an ungrateful child, for things that come easily are not valued very highly. Such parents often raise young husbands who buy what they please while their families are in need, or wives who ruin their husbands financially with their lust for material things. Allow your child the luxury of wanting something, waiting and planning for it, then working and saving for it. When he gets it he will be more inclined to thank the Lord for it, value it highly, and use it wisely. You will have done him a great favor.

Planning Their Life's Vocation

That title may be somewhat misleading, for it is not really our place to choose our child's occupation. Some parents have tried it. They have already decided that their children are going to follow in their footsteps or enter the family business. Others assume that their children are going on to college to prepare for some prestigious profession. Still others feel threatened by higher education and so pressure their children to choose a trade and start making a living. But we have no right to tell our children how God wants them to support themselves and their families. That decision is between them and the Lord. Our responsibility is to lead them to total commitment to Jesus Christ, then encourage them to seek his will in this most important decision of life.

From their earliest days our children should be assured that God has a plan for their lives, and that the very best kind of life requires finding and following that plan. Somehow or other too many kids have gotten the notion that God's path will be the most miserable, most difficult, and least rewarding way to go. So they decide to go their own way and do their own thing. But we can show them from Scripture, reinforced by illustrations from lives around us, that deciding for themselves is a dead-end street. "Before every man there lies a wide and pleasant road that seems right but ends in death."[10] Doing the will of God, on the other hand, brings joy and blessing.[11] At some point in their young lives they will need to yield themselves to Christ and say, "I want to follow his plan for my life." The example of our own submission to the will of God, in addition to the tender instruction we offer, will do much to bring them to this place of surrender to him.

Once that decision is made, the task of planning their life's vocation is greatly simplified. It is now a matter of helping them discover and do the will of God. Whatever they choose out of the thousands of job options open to them, it will be because God has called them to it and because it is the most strategic slot for them to use their God-given abilities for his glory. With that in mind, here are a few principles to guide you.

1. *Prayerfully look for their areas of interest and strength, then suggest ways to use them vocationally.* For instance, here is a boy with a keen interest in airplanes and an unusual aptitude for mechanics. Suggest something like, "You could make a great missionary pilot someday." God may use that seed thought to provide direction in years to come. Life is a drudgery when we are not doing what we like to do or what we are suited to do. God wants us where our talents will be utilized and our deepest longings satisfied.

2. *Expose them to outstanding Christians who have lived*

---

[10]Proverbs 14:12, TLB
[11]cf. James 1:25

their lives in the light of their commitment to Christ. Whether they are businessmen or missionaries, great athletes or great preachers, they will have a profound influence on your children. Their presence in your home and around your table will challenge your kids to make their lives count for Christ.

3. *Always hold out professional Christian service as a live option for your children.* While God needs committed Christians in every walk of life, the need for pastors, missionaries, and Christian educators is staggering. It certainly isn't God's will for every Christian to enter one of these professions. And they are no higher on God's scale than being his man or woman in the shop or office, if that is his will. But the overwhelming shortage of Christian workers would indicate that somebody isn't listening to God's call to vocational Christian service. Maybe parents are not talking about these needs nor emphasizing their utmost importance.

4. *Encourage your children to attend a good Christian school for at least one year.* No matter what vocation they believe God is leading them into, their courses in Bible, their contact with Christian leaders, and their opportunities for Christian service will help to make them more effective ambassadors of Jesus Christ for the rest of their lives.

Preparing Them for Marriage

The songwriter tells us that love and marriage go together like a horse and carriage. But to quote another old song, "It ain't necessarily so!" Some couples are at war. Their parents never did a thing to prepare them for the most intimate and important relationship of life. They may have actually given them a formula for failure by setting a faulty example. If we want to teach our little birds to fly right, we will need to grasp a few basic principles to guide us in training them for marriage.

1. *Be open and informal about sex from their earliest days.* Wholesome attitudes about sex are an indispensable ingredient of a happy marriage, and we implant those attitudes from their diaper days on. God designed sex as an important part of life, and the cost of ignorance about it is high—fear, humiliation, unwanted pregnancy, venereal disease, and broken homes.

Begin by calling parts of the body and bodily functions by their proper names. Camouflaging them with euphemisms passed down from one generation to the next implies that they are somehow shameful or dirty. And when the questions about sex begin to come, don't greet them with either shock or stony silence. In simple and direct language, tell the child what he wants to know and needs to know at his age. There is no need for an hour-long lecture on all the details of reproduction when your three-year-old asks where babies come from. But neither is there any excuse for a Christian parent to avoid the issue or fabricate some wild yarn. Tell him God makes the baby grow in a special place inside his mother. If he is inquisitive enough to ask how the baby got there in the first place, tell him daddy plants the seed there in love. The Bible isn't squeamish about the subject. Why should we be?

Our space is limited here, but a visit to your local Christian bookstore will not only uncover some excellent books to help you teach your children about sex, it will expose you to some excellent materials to put in their hands at each stage of their development, right up through marriage.

2. *Teach them their proper sexual roles in life.* Men are not superior to women as some would accuse the Bible of teaching but their functions are obviously different. God makes each of our children the sex he wants them to be for the unique job he wants them to accomplish in life. Instill in them a deep satisfaction for the role he has assigned them. Then explain to them the unusual changes that take place in their bodies at puberty

and how those changes fit into God's beautiful plan for them when they marry.

Mothers need to teach their daughters how to be good wives and homemakers, how to show their husbands their respect and admiration, and how to permeate the home with a cheerful spirit.[12] Fathers need to teach their sons to be good husbands, how to determine their wives' needs and meet them tenderly and unselfishly.[13] The best teacher is a good example. Mothers and fathers who engage in daily sparring matches or shouting meets will hardly rear good marriage partners.

3. *Show them how to find God's choice of a mate.* Although God calls some people to celibacy for special kinds of service, the normal pattern is to marry.[14] It is important for our children to know that if God wants them to marry, he has the perfect mate already picked out and in preparation somewhere in this world. Finding that very special one will result in their greatest possible joy. But how do they do it? They will begin by preparing themselves for the one of God's choosing, especially by cultivating a Christ-like character and an unselfish interest in others. Then they will look for opportunities to date as many different Christians as they can. If they begin going steady and limit themselves to one person too soon, they may never meet God's first choice. And if they date unbelievers, they expose themselves to the potential danger of an emotional involvement that will ultimately dishonor the Lord.

On their dates, they will maintain biblical standards and conduct themselves with purity. The sex drive is one of the most powerful forces in life, and it increases intensely before our children are ready to assume the responsibilities of marriage. When they get involved on a physical level they often allow themselves to be swept into marriage prematurely or with the wrong person, much to their deepening distress. So they must plan their dates purposely to avoid tempting situa-

[12]Ephesians 5:22-24, 33; Proverbs 31:10-31
[13]Ephesians 5:25-32
[14]Genesis 2:18

tions. And they must covenant with God that they will not kiss passionately, fondle each other's bodies, or do anything else that might lead them into sin. Mothers should explain to daughters how their manner of dress and conduct affects the opposite sex. Fathers should teach their sons to respect the personal dignity and sensitive feelings of the girls they date.

Furthermore, on their dates they will explore each other's personalities. Courting is not a device to win a mate by carefully masking our faults. It is a time to talk about areas of agreement and disagreement, to grapple with difficulties and work them out together by applying the principles of God's Word. The mate of God's choosing will not try to rationalize problems away, but will face them squarely and work at solving them biblically. As the right person emerges there will be a growing oneness of soul and spirit and a deepening bond of dedication to Christ. And when the crucial moment arrives, our little birds will be ready to fly. What a joyous day it will be when they give themselves to the mate of God's choice and begin to lay the foundations of a new godly generation. The loss we feel is more than compensated by our gratitude to God for his goodness and grace in bringing us successfully to this milestone.

4. *When they leave the nest, agree together on a few ground rules.* Some tense situations have arisen between parents and their married children because matters such as these were never discussed. For one thing, while you will always be available to help them when they need you, they basically are on their own. You will be delighted to offer advice on how to balance their budget, how to keep Sue's cake from flopping, how Sam can cope with his wife's moods, and similar problems. But the option of crying on mama's and daddy's shoulders after every little squabble is definitely not open to them.

For another thing, as grandparents you will thoroughly enjoy baby-sitting with your grandchildren, but you should not be taken advantage of. You do have your own lives to lead, and your lives should not revolve around those little ones, as precious as they are to you. You expect to be called far enough in advance to make the necessary plans, and you have the right to say "no" without lengthy explanations if you so desire.

Finally, there will be times when you will enjoy doing things for them and giving things to them. But you taught them how to work and how to handle their money. You will not permit them to sponge off you, nor should they expect you to bail them out of every financial scrape. You love them dearly and will pray for them faithfully, but they are no longer under your authority. You will respect that divine order of things and not interfere in their lives.[15] They should respect it and not allow themselves to remain dependent upon you any longer. They must learn to grow together in God's grace. And the joy of the Lord will be with you both.

---

[15]Genesis 2:24;
Matthew 19:5